The Pivot Point:
*Courage for the Change
You Secretly Want*

By
Lee Montajes

Lee Montajes

Copyright © 2025 Lee Montajes

All rights reserved.

No part of this publication may be reproduced, stored in a retrieval system, or transmitted in any form or by any means, electronic, mechanical, photocopying, recording, or otherwise, without prior written permission of the copyright owner, except in the case of brief quotations used in reviews or articles.

Dedication

To my Mum — Evelyn

Thank you for always believing in me. Even in moments of uncertainty as I transitioned careers and identities, you never stopped affirming me. You've been a steady reminder that life remains beautiful, even in the shadow of losing a great father. I love you deeply.

To Ryan — my husband

Despite our misunderstandings, you saw my determination. You stood by me through every high and low. Thank you for holding down the fort, especially with the kids, while I chased purpose. Your encouragement—and those healthy meals you prepare—fuel me more than you know. I couldn't have done this without you.

To Izzah Louise and Yumi Antoinnette

Thank you for your patience with my chaotic schedule as a nurse, educator, and now entrepreneur. You've witnessed the struggles, the triumphs, and the quiet battles—and still, you've loved me unconditionally.

"Sacrifice a little, success thereafter."

You've lived those words with me. Thank you for being my biggest cheerleaders.

To Lauren

You came into our lives with divine timing. When Grandpa Antonio Perez passed in 2017, you were born in 2018—unexpectedly, yet perfectly. You were the light after our loss. Your presence gave me strength to pivot with clarity and courage. You complete us.

To Geoff

As my second father, thank you for your unwavering love and support for me and our entire family. Your presence has been a blessing—a true pillar of strength and kindness. Love you so much.

Lee Montajes

To Izzy, Yumi, and Lauren

You've brought so much joy, hope, and abundance into our lives. You are my daily inspiration to keep showing up and giving my best.

To all my colleagues, family, friends, and business networks

Thank you for genuinely believing in me, encouraging my growth, and celebrating my achievements. You are precious gems in my life's journey.

To my social media family

Your loyalty means the world. You inspire me to keep showing up, to give back, and to speak light into others—every single day.

To all my critics

Thank you for the negative noise. I hope I've inspired you to keep going, even when the world says, "Stop."

Your resistance only sharpened my resolve.

To my father, Antonio Perez — in heaven

Even though your passing was the spark that ignited my journey as an entrepreneur, I carry you with me in every step I take. I hope you're proud of the woman I've become.

I wish you could've seen me grow into this purpose-driven life.

Thank you for teaching me humility, trustworthiness, empathy, courage, and the unwavering commitment to make a difference.

These values are the pillars of everything I do.

As an entrepreneur yourself, you didn't just teach—you walked the talk.

Love you so much Tatay (Dad)

We only live once.

Let's make it count—where our **passion** meets our **purpose.**
With all my love,
MotivationaLee

The Pivot Point: Courage for the Change You Secretly Want

Table of content

Dedication iii
Foreword 7
Introduction 9

Part One: The Restless Heart 12
Chapter 1: The Emptiness Behind the Mask 13
Chapter 2: Risk, Rain, and Red Soil 16
Chapter 3: The Critical Care Crisis That Changed Everything 21
Chapter 4: When Everything Looks Fine but Feels Wrong 26
Chapter 5: The Burnout You Don't Post About 31
Chapter 6: The Cost of Coping Too Well 36
Chapter 7: Grief, God, and a Hospital Bed: My Wake-Up Call 41
Chapter 8: Permission to Dream Again 46

Part Two: The Courage To Pivot 50
Chapter 9: Daring to Want More 51
Chapter 10: Letting Go of Titles, Holding On to Truth 56
Chapter 11: The Day I Chose Me 60
Chapter 12: Rebuilding From the Inside Out 66
Chapter 13: Critics, Comparisons, and Courage 71

Part Three: The Birth of a New Purpose 77
Chapter 14: From Nurse to Coach — A Story of Alignment 78
Chapter 15: From Grief to Grace — The Legacy of My Father 83
Chapter 16: The Unexpected Birth That Changed Everything 88
Chapter 17: What My Daughters Taught Me About Purpose 94
Chapter 18: The Business of Becoming You 98

Part Four: Living The Pivot Life 104
Chapter 19: How to Stay Rooted While You Rise 105

Chapter 20: Build a Life That Feels Good, Not Just Looks Good 109

Chapter 21: Reclaiming Your Power After Playing Small 113

Chapter 22: How I Found My Voice on Stage and Online 116

Chapter 23: Making Peace with Your Past to Step Into Your Future . 120

Part Five: Your Turn To Pivot 123

Chapter 24: The Pivot Plan – Mapping Your Path Forward 124

Chapter 25: Faith in Action – Spiritual Anchors in Times of Change 128

Chapter 26: The Five Saboteurs and How to Silence Them 132

Chapter 27: Small Steps, Big Shifts: How to Create Momentum 136

Chapter 28: From Fear to Fire – Becoming Who You Were Always Meant to Be 140

Chapter 29: The Power of Saying Yes to Yourself 144

Chapter 30: Becoming the Leader of Your Own Life 148

Conclusion: The Life That's Been Waiting for You 151

Acknowledgments 153

About the Author 156

Connect with Lee Montajes 158

The Pivot Point: Courage for the Change You Secretly Want

Foreword

By MotivationaLee

There comes a moment in life when everything you have built—your identity, your routine, your comfort zone—no longer feels like home. It can happen gradually, like the slow fading of a sunset, or suddenly, like the shattering sound of a breaking heart. For me, that moment was both a loss and a miracle.

In 2017, I lost my father. A gentle giant who stood by me through every season of life, his passing cracked something open in me. I thought grief would break me, but instead—it woke me up.

And then, in 2018, I gave birth to Lauren. At 43, I was placed in the high-risk category, but I was active, healthy, and grounded in my faith. Until the moment that changed everything. Shortly after a normal delivery, I began to haemorrhage—a massive, life-threatening bleed. I lost more than a third of my blood volume. I remember the chaos, the Code Blue, the rush of medical staff, the urgency in their voices:

"Lee, keep breathing. Just stay awake!"

I felt my consciousness slipping. But even in the blur, I chose surrender, not fear. I whispered to God:

"If You let me go, I'm ready to see my dad. But if You let me live, I promise to use everything You've given me—for others."

As I was wheeled into the operating theatre, I began to sing through my spirit:

"Lord, I offer my life to You… Mighty to save…"

I came back. Not just from the brink of death—but into a life I could finally live with truth, freedom, and full expression. That moment became my pivot point.

This book was born from that sacred promise.

The Pivot Point is not just a collection of stories or strategies. It is a soul map for anyone who has ever stood on the edge of change and wondered if they were brave enough to leap. It is for the woman who feels invisible behind her responsibilities. For the man who has built a life that looks successful but feels empty. For the dreamer who buried their voice because reality seemed louder than hope.

Inside these pages, I share my most vulnerable truths—not as someone who has it all figured out, but as someone who has chosen to keep becoming.

You will find stories that will stir your heart, questions that will challenge your comfort, and affirmations that will anchor you in courage. This is not just a book you read. It is a journey you take.

If you have ever felt the call for more—more meaning, more alignment, more you—then consider this your divine permission slip.

Your pivot point is not the end. It is the beginning of your most powerful, purposeful life.

Let us begin—

MotivationaLee

Introduction

The Pivot Point: Courage for the Change You Secretly Want

The Quiet Nudge Towards Change

*"There comes a moment when staying the same becomes more painful than the fear of change.
That moment is your pivot point."
— MotivationaLee*

We don't always recognise turning points as they're happening.

Sometimes, they arrive disguised as heartbreak.

Other times, as a health scare. A quiet surrender. A loss so deep that you are never quite the same.

For me, there were two such moments.

The First Pivot: When My Father Died

My father wasn't just family—he was a grounding force.

When he passed, something cracked open in me.

Suddenly, I was flooded with questions:

- What legacy am I building?
- What truly matters in the end?
- Am I living in a way that would make him proud—and that honours the shortness of this precious life?

The Second Pivot: Life After the Bleeding

I was 43, pregnant with my youngest daughter, Lauren.

Despite my age, I was healthy, strong, and filled with life. The delivery went smoothly.

But the moment the placenta was delivered, everything changed.

A massive postpartum haemorrhage took over.

In just minutes, I lost over a third of my blood. I heard the urgent panic around me:

"Code blue!"

"Lee, keep breathing. Stay with us!"

Then, the rush to the operating theatre.

I was slipping. Weakening. Fading.

And in that sacred in-between space—between life and death—I surrendered.

I whispered a prayer:

"Lord, take care of my family. Let Your will be done."

And then I sang:

🎵 "Lord, I Offer My Life to You"

🎵 "Mighty to Save"

There was no fear.

No resistance.

Only faith.

And in that moment, I made a silent vow:

"If You let me live, I'll use my life for Your glory. I'll speak. I'll coach. I'll write. I'll step fully into the gifts You've given me—and help others do the same."

I woke up groggy but alive.

The surgery was successful. The medical team told me they'd heard me praying in tongues.

I told them, "I was only singing."

But deep down, I knew: something divine had passed through that room.

This Was My Pivot Point

It wasn't just a new chapter—it was a new calling.

This book is my story.

The Pivot Point: Courage for the Change You Secretly Want

But more than that, it's a mirror for your story.

It's for the woman who's followed all the rules, done all the right things, and still feels there's something more.

It's for the strong ones.

The silent strugglers.

The burnt-out high achievers.

The quietly brave dreamers.

Each chapter is a truth I learned the hard way.

Each one will guide you through your own pivots:

- From burnout to balance
- From performing to purpose
- From fear to full aliveness

You don't need a tragedy to change your life.

But you do need a truth bold enough to wake you up.

This Is Your Invitation

To answer the whisper within.

The one that's been saying:

"It's time."

Time to stop shrinking.

Time to reclaim your voice.

Time to use your gifts.

Time to step into the life you were meant to live.

Let's begin—your pivot point is waiting.

Let's begin—together.

Part One:
The Restless Heart

Chapter 1:
The Emptiness Behind the Mask

Original Quote:

"Success without purpose is the loudest silence you'll ever hear." — MotivationaLee

I had a good life in the Philippines—a stable job and a balanced lifestyle. On the surface, everything seemed fine. But deep inside, there was a quiet restlessness, a longing to live with deeper purpose. Something felt missing.

In my home country, success is often defined by status. You earn more respect and admiration if you're a Doctor, Lawyer, Engineer, or Nurse. Titles carry weight, and people tend to look up to you based on your profession. But for me, it felt limiting. I didn't feel like I truly belonged. I couldn't fully be myself in the long term. I was expected to fit a mould, to meet expectations that didn't align with the person I was becoming.

I've always believed that life is more than just a job title or a pay cheque. Self-actualisation—becoming the best version of myself while staying true to my mission as a Nurse—was what truly mattered to me. I wanted to be in a place where I could be free to be myself. A place where I could be happy and make a difference, regardless of professional or financial status.

Back in the 1990s, becoming a Life Coach was unheard of. It was considered strange—even laughable. Some would joke, "A coach? Like for basketball?" But deep down, I knew it was a calling. I just needed the right environment to nurture it.

For years, I waited for a chance to leave my comfort zone, believing I would eventually go to America—the typical Filipino dream. But life surprised me with a detour. Instead of the U.S., I ended up in the United Kingdom.

Letting go and trusting in God, I believed that my purpose would unfold through my nursing journey. The transition wasn't easy—new culture, new systems, new accents, new people. But within a year, I found myself fully immersed and unexpectedly feeling at home. The people in Great Britain were kind, thoughtful, and accepting.

I moved through the stages of culture shock—honeymoon, frustration, adaptation, and finally, acceptance. And what I found here was more than just a new chapter. I found alignment.

Here, I don't need a title to prove my worth. There's no pressure to maintain a certain image. I'm free to speak, sing, coach, and serve—often pro bono—because it's not about prestige. It's about purpose.

No status. No ego. Just authenticity, contribution, and joy.

Strategy Spotlight: Navigating Major Life Transitions

- **Listen to the Inner Stirring** – The voice urging you for more isn't random. It's your soul's compass.
- **Let Go of "How It Should Look"** – Detours often carry divine redirection. Don't resist them.
- **Prepare for Cultural Transitions** – Study, listen, adapt, and connect. It helps you move from surviving to thriving.
- **Stay Purpose-Aligned** – In every new place, ask: How can I live my values here?
- **Use Your Gifts Everywhere** – Don't wait for a stage or title. Start where you are, with what you have.

Reflection Questions

- What inner longing have you been silencing due to fear of judgement or unfamiliarity?
- How have life's detours shaped your direction in unexpected ways?
- Where in your current life can you be more authentic and aligned with your values?

The Pivot Point: Courage for the Change You Secretly Want

Key Affirmation:

"I trust the detours of my life. Every transition is preparing me for a deeper purpose." Motivationalee

Key Takeaways

- Self-actualisation often begins where comfort ends.
- Purpose transcends geography, status, and even logic.
- True success is found where your soul feels seen, not where your title sounds prestigious.
- It's okay to want more—even when everything seems "good enough."
- Detours are not distractions; they're directions in disguise.

Action Step

Write a "Culture Transition Letter" to your past self. Reassure them that they're on the right path, and that the unfamiliar place they fear may be the very space where their purpose will flourish.

Chapter 2:
Risk, Rain, and Red Soil

In November 2009, we moved to Adelaide, Australia, during the height of the world's credit crunch. Back in the UK, the National Health Service (NHS) was slowly collapsing under financial strain. Wards were closing. Staff were being redeployed to unfamiliar units. Uncertainty was everywhere.

I could see the signs. It wasn't safe anymore—not just financially, but emotionally. The stability we once knew in the UK was slipping away. I thought of Canada first, then America. But both countries had long visa waiting times—up to two years. Australia, however, seemed like the only country down under that wasn't crushed by the global crisis.

I wasn't even sure why Australia felt like the right choice. It seemed like a divine nudge—an invisible pull from God. What was His plan? Why this sudden redirection? It felt radical, uncertain, and hopeful all at once. We applied for a work sponsorship visa, and within a week, it was granted. That quick approval felt like a sign. Since I was a British citizen, the transition in terms of paperwork was smooth. Australia, like the UK, it is a Commonwealth country, and the healthcare system, particularly the operating theatre protocols and bedside care, closely mirrored the UK's standards.

So, we packed up our lives and left everything familiar behind. We had no family, no close friends in Adelaide. It was just us—my husband, our two toddlers, and me.

Thanks to Yahoo Chat (yes, good old Yahoo!), I connected with a kind stranger who offered to help. When we landed, we had to move from one house to another before we met a wonderful couple—Rosalie, a Filipino woman, and her British husband, Bryan. They welcomed us like family and let us stay in their home for over a month until we found our own place near my workplace. With our two little ones, we rented just one room for the four of us.

The Pivot Point: Courage for the Change You Secretly Want

Once we moved out of their house, we had no furniture—nothing but bare walls and empty space. I still hadn't received my first pay cheque. We slept on the floor using cardboard as mattress padding, and an unused operating theatre drape as a makeshift blanket. Carole McCaw and Geoff, colleagues from work, lent us bed sheets. Craig and his wife shared their extra cutlery and kitchen tools. We were strangers in a foreign land, yet kindness met us at every turn.

We walked everywhere—sometimes 5 to 8 kilometres in the scorching 48–50°C Adelaide summer heat. With no car and no TV, our kids asked, "Mum, are we poor?" I laughed it off. All we had was a tiny black-and-white television we picked up from a kerbside rubbish collection in an affluent suburb. Eventually, we also picked up a microwave the same way and bought a vacuum cleaner and washing machine from a second-hand shop. In Great Britain, we had a big, comfortable TV—yet none of that mattered now. This was the beginning of something new.

Life was quiet in Adelaide. I missed the city buzz of the UK. At night, you could hear the chirping of crickets—so still, so unfamiliar. I questioned if I had made the right decision. Was this truly God's plan? Still, I held on to faith. I believed something big was waiting for us here.

At work, I had to leave the house at 5:00 a.m. just to catch two buses and arrive on time for a 7:00 a.m. shift. This was while we were still living with Rosalie and Bryan. The commute took an hour and a half across two buses, and while it was a sacrifice, I strangely enjoyed it. It gave me time to pray, reflect, and let my mind wander into creative thinking.

Some days, I was called in for emergency operations, and I'd look up at the early morning sky with tears in my eyes, silently praying:

"Until when, Lord? I want to be more… but thank You for this job."

Still, I remained grateful for this unplanned adventure. It was tough, yes—but it was also fun. I looked forward to whatever the future might unfold. I knew I could always return to the UK if I needed to anyway.

Within less than six months, we were financially stable. We were able to buy furniture and essential household items. We met more friends—Filipinos and other multicultural families. Our circle grew. We served in the parish: I as a Lector, my husband as a Lay Minister, and our kids as altar servers.

Looking back now, my kids—now grown—often talk about those early days. Sleeping on cardboard, walking in the heat, sharing one room. It taught them humility and the value of resilience. They saw that Mum never gave up.

Those humble beginnings became our foundation. We started from scratch, yes—but we never complained. We didn't expect handouts. We were simply grateful. Grateful for the British-Aussie friends who celebrated our first Christmas and New Year with us in this new land.

Australia wasn't in the plan—but it was part of God's plan. We thought it would be just two years. Yet here we are. Still standing. Still rising.

Strategies & Tips for Navigating Radical Transitions

- **Trust the Nudge**: If you feel a strong urge to act or move, don't dismiss it. Journal through it and take one small step toward the possibility.
- **Be Resourceful**: Pick second-hand items, accept help, and repurpose creatively. Humble beginnings are not failures—they are springboards.
- **Build a Support Network**: Connect with local community groups, online forums, or faith-based communities. These can anchor you emotionally during transition.
- **Keep a Gratitude Ritual**: Even in the hardest moments, write down three things you're grateful for every day. It rewires your resilience.
- **Let Faith Frame Your Future**: Whether spiritual or philosophical, hold on to a belief that your story isn't over—it's just unfolding.

The Pivot Point: Courage for the Change You Secretly Want

Reflection Questions

- Have you ever started over in a completely unfamiliar place? What did it teach you?
- In what areas of your life are you currently relying on faith or trust in the unknown?
- Who showed up for you when you had nothing—and how have you passed that kindness forward?

Key Affirmation:

"I honour my humble beginnings. Every step, every sacrifice has shaped my strength, and my future is full of promise." Motivationalee

Key Takeaways

- Starting over is scary, but sometimes it's the only way to create something better.
- Being resourceful and staying grateful can transform even the most difficult beginnings.
- Humble beginnings plant the seeds of resilience, appreciation, and deep character.
- You don't need everything figured out to start. You just need courage and a bit of faith.
- Even strangers can become the family you didn't know you needed.

Action Steps

- **Document Your Journey**: Write down the milestones of your own humble beginnings. Reflect on how far you've come.
- **Stay Grateful**: Make a gratitude list of things you once considered challenges but now see as blessings.
- **Be the Stranger Who Helps**: Pay forward the kindness you received. Offer help to someone who's new or struggling.

- **Start With What You Have**: Don't wait for perfect conditions. Build with what's in your hands now.
- **Carve Out Thinking Time**: Use commute time or quiet moments for reflection, dreaming, or prayer—it can lead to breakthroughs.

Sometimes, our deepest transformation happens in the places we didn't plan to go.

Sometimes, the very soil that feels most unfamiliar is the one that will teach us how to bloom in ways we never imagined.

Chapter 3:
The Critical Care Crisis That Changed Everything

Original Quote:

"When life places you in a crisis, it's not to crush you—but to reveal the power you forgot you had." — MotivationaLee

You Never Forget the Smell of Adrenaline

In the operating theatre, it clings to the air—tangy and sterile. Time does not flow there; it pulses. It is a place where life and death hold hands, where every second counts, and every breath could be someone's last.

I was at the peak of my nursing career. Confident. Competent. In control.

But it was within that control that the first crack appeared.

One day, a patient came in—a mother, not unlike me. Late thirties. No pre-existing conditions. She had just given birth and suffered a sudden, catastrophic postpartum haemorrhage. Her blood pressure dropped. Her organs began shutting down. She was clinging to life.

I was assigned to her case.

As I stood over her, adjusting the IV lines, titrating vasopressors, preparing to intubate, my hands moved with clinical precision. But inside—something was unravelling.

This could have been me.

Just months before, I had also given birth. I had also faced complications. I had bled too. I had prayed desperately, "God, not now. My daughter needs me."

And now, this woman's fight for life mirrored my own—except she wasn't waking up.

The Collapse Behind the Curtain

That shift was the beginning of my own internal emergency.

On the outside, I kept showing up. I was the strong one. The calm in chaos. The voice of assurance to anxious families.

But inside?

I was breaking.

I began waking in the middle of the night, drenched in sweat. Flashbacks from work bled into my dreams. I would hear the beeping of monitors even at home. My heart would race with no warning, and I began to fear the sound of silence.

One evening, after yet another exhausting shift, I sat alone in my car and wept uncontrollably. Not from fatigue—but from a soul-deep emptiness.

What is happening to me?

This wasn't burnout. This was something deeper. A reckoning.

I had built my identity around saving lives. But no one had ever taught me how to save my own.

The Day I Broke (and Breathed Again)

The breaking point came unexpectedly—during a code blue.

The patient didn't make it. I had done everything—everything—but the life slipped away.

As I walked out of the room, my knees buckled. I leaned against the corridor wall and slid to the floor.

No one noticed.

And in that moment, I realised I had become invisible—even to myself.

That night, I went home, looked in the mirror, and didn't recognise the woman staring back.

That was when I heard the whisper again:

The Pivot Point: Courage for the Change You Secretly Want

There is more.

Not just more *for* me. But more that I was meant to *give*. Just not here. Not like this.

The Shift from Care to Calling

I began exploring what healing might look like beyond the hospital walls. I started journalling, reading about purpose, psychology, and coaching. I prayed. I cried. I resisted.

Because walking away from something you're good at can feel like betrayal.

But I didn't yet understand that I wasn't walking away—I was stepping forward. Into something deeper. Something that would allow me to use my experience in a way that didn't destroy me.

Eventually, I made the decision that terrified me the most:

I walked away from clinical nursing.

Not because I had stopped caring.

But because I had started listening—to myself, to my spirit, to the ache in my chest that had gone ignored for too long.

That decision wasn't easy. It felt like a death. But it was also a birth—the beginning of a calling that would lead me to become a speaker, a coach, an educator, and eventually, an author.

Strategies and Insights

- **Crisis Reveals Truth**: What breaks you open often leads you to the truth of who you are. Do not run from the breaking.
- **Your Pain Has Purpose**: The moments that hurt the most may one day become the foundation of your mission.
- **Redefine What It Means to Help**: Sometimes, helping others means healing yourself first—so you can serve from overflow, not depletion.

Reflection Questions

- Have you ever reached a breaking point that forced you to question your identity or career?
- What moments in your life have brought you closer to your true calling—even if they came wrapped in pain?
- Where are you still pretending to be "fine", when your spirit is asking for something more?

Key Affirmation:

"I honour the breaking, because it opened the door to my becoming. I no longer hide in crisis—I rise from it." Motivationalee

Key Takeaways

- **Crisis Is a Catalyst for Clarity**: Life-altering moments often feel like breakdowns, but they carry the seeds of breakthrough. Crisis strips away illusion and forces us to see what truly matters.
- **You Can't Pour From an Empty Cup**: True leadership and caregiving begin with self-leadership. If you're burned out, numb, or silently suffering, it's not weakness—it's a signal to pause and repair.
- **Your Healing Journey Is Part of Your Legacy**: The pain you survive is not wasted. It becomes wisdom, empathy, and depth that you carry into every future calling.
- **Leaving Isn't Quitting—It's Choosing Yourself**: Walking away from a career you've mastered doesn't mean failure; it means choosing alignment, peace, and purpose over performance and survival.
- **Identity Can Be Rebuilt from the Rubble**: When your professional role collapses, your worth doesn't disappear. What's left is the raw material of reinvention.

The Pivot Point: Courage for the Change You Secretly Want

Action Steps

- **Name Your Inner Emergency**: Write a journal entry as if you were your own patient. What vital signs are you ignoring?

- **Choose One Boundary**: If you are in a high-stress profession, choose one healthy boundary this week that protects your emotional wellbeing.

- **Create a "Healing Résumé"**: List experiences—not just qualifications—that shaped your wisdom. What have you lived through that could help someone else?

What broke you wasn't meant to end you. It was meant to awaken you.

Chapter 4:
When Everything Looks Fine but Feels Wrong

Original Quote:

"You can have a life that looks successful on the outside and still feel like you're suffocating on the inside. That's not failure—it's a whisper from your soul asking for something more."
— MotivationaLee

I Had Ticked All the Boxes

Career? Tick.

Respect? Tick.

A beautiful family? Tick.

An award-winning professional life in nursing and education? Double tick.

From the outside, I was living what many would call a "dream life." I was the one people came to for advice. I was the leader, the mentor, the calm in the Critical Care storm, the educator of future nurses. I was the strong one.

But inside, something was off.

It wasn't burnout—at least, not yet. It was subtler than that. A slow erosion of joy. A quiet ache that whispered in the spaces between the busyness. A strange hollowness that crept in during moments that should have felt fulfilling.

At first, I ignored it.

I called it tiredness. Blamed hormones. Justified it with the weight of responsibility. After all, when you've spent decades mastering your craft, raising a family, and showing up for everyone else—how dare you question the life you've worked so hard to build?

But the discontent grew louder.

The Pivot Point: Courage for the Change You Secretly Want

It surfaced in the silence after a speech. In the lonely drive home after another packed day. In the pause between the applause and the quiet question: *Is this really it?*

I didn't hate my life—I just couldn't *feel* it anymore. I'd become so used to being "on" that I didn't even realise I'd disconnected from myself.

And then, one day, I broke down—in the middle of what should have been a proud moment.

I'd just delivered a high-stakes professional development session. One I'd done a hundred times before. Applause. Compliments. Emails flooding my inbox.

But I felt... nothing. No joy. No fulfilment. Just numb.

That night, I sat in my car, gripping the steering wheel as tears streamed down my face. I felt ungrateful. Ashamed. Confused.

Why wasn't this enough?

Why didn't I feel the satisfaction I used to?

That moment marked the beginning of my unravelling—and, eventually, my awakening.

The Truth Behind the Smile

Women—especially those in leadership and caregiving roles—are taught to carry it all gracefully. We're taught to measure our worth by our output. Our appearances. The applause.

And we wear our success like armour, even when it's quietly cracking beneath the surface.

There's a particular kind of grief that comes with realising the life you've built no longer fits the woman you've become.

But most of us are too afraid to say it out loud.

So, we shrink. We stay. We keep performing. We convince ourselves it's just a phase. Just a rough season.

Until the ache becomes too loud to ignore.

For me, that ache was a holy discomfort—one that led me to a new chapter I didn't know I needed.

I didn't have a clear plan. Only a feeling. A deep, soul-level unrest that whispered:

This isn't the end of your story. It's the beginning of your becoming.

Strategy Spotlight: Navigating Internal Dissatisfaction

- **Listen to Your Inner Discomfort** – When things feel off, don't dismiss the feeling. It's your soul's way of signaling that something is misaligned.
- **Give Yourself Permission to Question** – It's okay to ask, "*Is this really the life I want, even if it looks perfect* on *the outside?*"
- **Slow Down to Hear Your Truth** – Take time each day to reflect and ask yourself if you're truly fulfilled, or just going through the motions.
- **Embrace the Quiet Moments** – Sometimes, discontent comes in stillness. Allow these moments of discomfort to guide your decisions moving forward.
- **Align Actions with Values** – Reassess your daily choices. Are they in line with your core beliefs? If not, start making adjustments.

Reflection Questions

- Have you ever found yourself living a life that looked successful on the outside but felt hollow on the inside?
- What signs is your body, mind, or spirit giving you that something needs to shift?
- What would you do if you weren't afraid of disappointing others?
- Where in your life are you performing instead of being?

The Pivot Point: Courage for the Change You Secretly Want

Key Affirmation:

"I honour the whisper within me that says there is more. I choose authenticity over approval, truth over performance, and alignment over applause." Motivationalee

Key Takeaways

- A life that *looks* good on the outside does not always *feel* good on the inside—and that doesn't mean you're broken.
- Discontent is often a divine nudge, not a breakdown.
- The first step towards change is recognising misalignment—and being honest with yourself about it.
- You do not need to wait for a crisis to grant yourself permission to pivot. Sometimes, clarity begins in the quiet ache.

Action Steps

- **Create a "Truth Journal"** – For the next 7 days, write one sentence a day beginning with: *"If I were being completely honest with myself, I'd admit that..."*
- **Rate Your Alignment** – On a scale of 1–10, how aligned do you feel in your work, relationships, and personal life? Anything under a 7 is worth exploring.
- **Tell One Trusted Person** – Share your truth with someone safe. Speaking it out loud dissolves shame and invites support.
- **Schedule Stillness** – Give yourself 10 minutes of daily quiet to hear your own voice. You might be surprised what rises.
- **Unfollow the "Shoulds"** – Identify one "should" you're living by that no longer fits—and choose to release it.

This was just the beginning of my story, but it was the most important moment. The day I admitted something felt wrong—even when everything looked right—was the day I chose myself.

It was the moment I cracked open the door to possibility.

And in the chapters ahead, I'll walk you through the heartbreak, the courage, the breakthroughs, and the rebirth that followed.

Because on the other side of honesty… is freedom.

The Pivot Point: Courage for the Change You Secretly Want

- True leadership includes leading yourself with care, compassion, and boundaries.

Action Steps:

- **Audit Your Energy:** List out your weekly responsibilities. Which ones drain you? Which ones refill you?
- **Schedule Rest Like It Matters:** Block out time for recovery. Not as a luxury, but as a necessity.
- **Communicate Your Limits:** Be honest with your team and family about what you can realistically take on.
- **Seek Support:** Burnout thrives in isolation. Talk to a mentor, coach, or therapist.
- **Redefine Success:** Write a new definition of success that includes your health, relationships, and inner peace.

You are not a machine. You are a masterpiece.

You were not created to run on empty.

The pivot often begins in the silence after collapse.

That's where the whisper of a new life begins.

Let's keep going.

Chapter 6:
The Cost of Coping Too Well

A True Story of Silent Burnout During the COVID Lockdowns

During Melbourne's lockdowns, I did what many educators and healthcare professionals did — I adapted. I adjusted. I pushed on.

As a Nurse Educator and Lecturer, I taught full-time online, supporting students virtually while also preparing to return to campus for essential practical sessions.

Flexibility was expected, and I delivered. But no one warns you that constant flexibility can slowly erode your foundation.

My days were packed: virtual lectures, endless emails, and comforting students facing uncertainty, illness, and fear. I was "on" all the time. If I wasn't teaching, I was marking. If I wasn't marking, I was planning. And when I wasn't planning, I was worrying about how to help those struggling silently on the other side of the screen.

Then came the in-person sessions: lab demonstrations, back-to-back, with small, spaced-out groups. I repeated the same lesson every hour, again and again. I kept smiling. I kept going.

And then the OSCEs.

If a student failed their first attempt, I reshuffled my schedule to give them a second chance. If another was unwell or struggling with mental health, I made space for them too. That's what we do. We make space. For everyone but ourselves.

It wasn't just the workload — it was the emotional labour. I held space for their stress and fear but left none for my own.

I told myself, I'm fine. I'm healthy. I'm managing.

Until one day, my body told a different story.

The Pivot Point: Courage for the Change You Secretly Want

The Moment Everything Shifted

It started with a wave of dizziness. I figured I was just dehydrated or had low blood sugar. I brushed it off. I was walking down the stairs at home — something I'd done a thousand times — and then suddenly...

I couldn't move.

My body froze.

Before I could process it, my legs gave way and I fell down the last five steps.

I didn't lose consciousness. I wasn't confused. But I felt helpless. My critical care nurse brain switched on: Is it neurological? Spinal? A torn ligament? I lay there, bruised and stunned, alone.

I called out for help, but no one was home.

With effort, I dragged myself up with my arms. Crawling. Slowly. Carefully. Back to the room where my laptop was still open. The class was still running. It was activity time — nearly the end of a three-hour session.

And what did I do? What so many educators do.

I didn't say a word.

I turned on my camera. I smiled. I wrapped up the class like nothing had happened.

No one knew I had just crawled back into frame.

The Cost of Silence

Moments later, my mum and little one came home. She took one look at me and panicked. She wanted to call an ambulance. I told her I was fine. Not because I was, but because I didn't want to trigger her anxiety.

I asked for a gram of paracetamol. Then I did what nurses do best: I assessed myself.

Vitals: normal. Pain: manageable. Urgency: low.

I triaged myself. I wasn't an emergency. I didn't want to spend hours in ED. So I booked an after-hours doctor and made a GP appointment for the next day.

At the GP, I listed all the possibilities: musculoskeletal trauma, slipped disc, nerve impingement. I was overthinking. Overanalysing. Exactly what Type A people do when they finally

stop moving.

She listened carefully and then said:

"Lorilee, you're healthy. But this is over-fatigue. Your body shut down before you gave yourself permission to stop."

I was stunned.

I thought I was managing. I ate well. Exercised. Slept enough — or so I thought. I did everything "right." But burnout doesn't always look obvious, especially in Type A personalities. We don't always look unwell. We don't always show the signs. We just keep going — until something gives.

I had been coping so well I didn't realise I was burning out.

I thought my dedication would protect me.

But behind the dedication was overextension, isolation, depletion.

We say, I'm just busy.

But what we really mean is: I'm barely holding it all together.

In education and healthcare, burnout is normalised. We wear it like a badge of honour. But it's not a rite of passage. It's a warning sign.

When Burnout Wears a Smile

It hit me hard.

I thought I was safe because I ate healthy. Exercised. Meditated. Planned everything. But even healthy routines can hide the symptoms.

Even strong people can fall.

The Pivot Point: Courage for the Change You Secretly Want

Even high-performers can crash — not because they're weak, but because they keep going when they should have stopped.

Type A personalities are especially at risk. We're efficient. Disciplined. We hide struggle with structure. We power through the warning signs. Until our body forces us to listen.

Burnout doesn't always look like collapse. Sometimes, it looks like dedication.

It sounds like I ended up off work for nearly three months. Not because I chose to rest — but because I had to heal.

Healing wasn't easy. It was uncomfortable. Vulnerable. Necessary.

But it was also transformative.

Three Months Off. Not by Choice — But by Necessity.

I was forced to take nearly three months off. Not for a holiday — for healing.

In that space, I learned burnout doesn't always come with flashing lights. Sometimes it arrives in silence. In numbness. In stillness you didn't choose.

Even healthy habits can't outrun emotional depletion.

Even resilience has its breaking point.

Strategies & Insights

- Recognise early signs: trouble sleeping, short temper, physical fatigue, constant busyness.
- Pace yourself after peak periods: OSCEs, marking seasons, teaching marathons.
- Set energy boundaries, not just time boundaries. Ask: Does this nourish or drain me?
- Create a recovery rhythm: daily decompression, weekly reflection, quarterly reset.

- Speak the truth: I need help. I need rest. I'm not okay. — without guilt.

Reflective Questions
- What signs does my body give me when I'm nearing burnout?
- Where am I over-functioning to hide how I'm really feeling?
- What would it look like to be supported instead of stretched?
- Who do I trust enough to talk to before I hit breaking point?

Key Affirmation:

"I honour my limits. Rest is not weakness — it's wisdom. I choose to care for myself with the same compassion I give to others." Motivationalee

Key Takeaway

Burnout isn't proof you're broken. It's proof you've been strong for too long.

You don't have to collapse to deserve rest.

Your body will whisper before it screams. Listen early.

Action Steps

1. Schedule protected "unavailable" time weekly — even 15 minutes can make a difference.
2. Start a Burnout Tracker — check in daily on energy, mood, physical cues.
3. Reframe rest as responsibility, not reward.
4. Normalise speaking up — role model it in your team or classroom.
5. Make recovery part of your workflow — not just what happens after crisis.

Chapter 7:
Grief, God, and a Hospital Bed:
My Wake-Up Call

Original Quote:

"Sometimes, it takes a breaking point for your soul to rise and remember why it came here."
— *MotivationaLee*

There are moments that divide time.

Before.

And after.

For me, it was the day I found myself in a hospital bed—not as a nurse, not as an educator, not as the composed woman others leaned on—but as a patient.

A woman in crisis. Forced to stop.

I was 43, pregnant with my daughter, Lauren. That season was both sacred and terrifying. I was older, wiser, and all too aware of how fragile life could be. After decades in critical care, I had witnessed life begin and end countless times. Yet nothing prepared me for what it felt like when my own body gave way.

The collapse was swift. My body weakened, the room spun, and suddenly, I was no longer the one caring for others—I was the one being cared for.

The Sacred Pause

I do not know how long I was unconscious. What I do remember is the stillness when I woke: clarity, reverence, and a strange peace.

I had survived.

But more than that—I had been stopped in my tracks.

That bed became more than a hospital bed. It became a sacred pause. A line in the sand.

Not just to live, but to live differently.

I realized how much of my life had been spent hustling for worth, performing excellence, chasing approval. I had been so busy performing life that I had forgotten to live it.

When Grief Meets God

In that fragile season, gratitude and grief lived side by side.

Grief for the years I spent proving myself.

Grief for the moments I missed while chasing perfection.

Grief for the version of me who thought love had to be earned through performance.

But it was in that grief that God met me.

Not in a lightning bolt.

Not with a booming voice.

But in grace.

In the warmth of my daughter's skin.

In the steady hand of the midwife beside me.

In the quiet whisper: *"You're still here, because there's more."*

This wasn't just about physical survival. It was a spiritual awakening.

The Realignment Begins

From that moment, I could not return to who I had been.

Something had shifted. A holy discomfort. A pull toward purpose.

I began to ask new questions:

- Why am I truly here?
- What legacy am I building?
- What do I want my children to remember about their mother?

The Pivot Point: Courage for the Change You Secretly Want

- More importantly—what do I want to remember about myself?

That hospital bed became an altar. A place where the old me was laid to rest, and a new version of me began to rise—not with certainty, but with courage.

It was not the final pivot. That would come later.

But it was the beginning of a realignment.

That bed broke me.

But it also birthed me.

And in **Chapter 16**, I return to this very moment—the day that stopped me in my tracks—to share how grief, faith, and purpose reshaped my life in ways I never imagined.

Strategy Spotlight: Transforming Grief into Growth

- **Reframe Grief as a Catalyst** – See grief as an invitation to transformation, not just a painful ending.

- **Honour the Emotional Journey** – Don't rush through grief. Let it guide you toward healing.

- **Create Space for Reflection** – Use quiet time to realign your life with what truly matters.

- **Release What No Longer Serves You** – Let go of outdated roles and pressures, clearing space for new growth.

- **Find Meaning in the Pain** – Ask, "What is this moment teaching me about resilience and purpose?"

Reflection Questions

- Have you ever experienced a moment that forced you to pause?

- What areas of your life feel misaligned, even if you've tolerated them?

- What would your life look like if you began honouring what truly matters?
- Where have you been performing instead of surrendering?

Key Affirmation

"I choose to live a life that reflects my soul, not just my schedule. I surrender to what matters and rise into who I was born to be." — MotivationaLee

Key Takeaways

- Crisis can be a doorway to calling—if we listen.
- Surrender is not weakness; it is sacred strength.
- Grief can open the path to grace.
- Life will not wait for us to feel ready—but it will always respond to our willingness.

Action Steps

1. **Create Your "Before and After" Timeline** – Identify a life-altering moment. Write about who you were before—and who you became after.
2. **Practise Daily Surrender** – Each morning, take three quiet minutes to say: "I surrender today. Lead me."
3. **Name What Matters Most** – Write down your five core values. Are you living them—or just believing in them?
4. **Release What's No Longer Yours** – Choose one outdated expectation or role you've outgrown. Bless it, then begin to release it.
5. **Make a Gratitude-Grit List** – List three moments where you were held by grace—when you thought you would not make it, but did.

The Pivot Point: Courage for the Change You Secretly Want

That hospital bed was not just about loss. It was about realignment.

I lost time, but I gained vision.

I was shaken, but I was awakened.

That day did not define me—it refined me.

And it became the quiet prelude to an even bigger awakening still to come.

Chapter 8:
Permission to Dream Again

Original Quote:

"You don't need a breakdown to earn your breakthrough. You only need permission—from yourself—to dream again."
MotivationaLee

There's a quiet moment, often overlooked, between exhaustion and awakening. It's the space where your soul dares to whisper, *"What if there's more?"*

For years, I silenced that voice. I called it fantasy. Naïveté. Immaturity.

"Be grateful," I'd tell myself. *"You have a career. A title. A good income. Security."*

But beneath that gratitude was mourning—a future I no longer believed was mine.

The Weight of Responsibility

I spent years as a theatre nurse before moving into education and leadership. I was respected, capable, reliable.

But I wasn't free.

I'd become an expert at carrying other people's emergencies, expectations and dreams—while neglecting my own. I operated with excellence, but my heart was running on empty.

I began to wonder:

- What happened to the girl who wrote poems and short stories by candlelight?
- What happened to the woman who lit up when she spoke—not just about pathophysiology, but about purpose?
- Where was the woman who dreamed without limits?

I'd buried her under layers of duty.

The Pivot Point: Courage for the Change You Secretly Want

Then one day, I saw her again—in my daughter's eyes.

She was sketching, colouring wildly outside the lines. When I asked what she was drawing, she said confidently:

"My future. I'm making up my own job."

That moment cracked something open in me. I realised children don't ask for permission to dream.

Somewhere along the way, we learn to beg for it.

We ask for permission to want more.

To speak up.

To slow down.

To change direction.

To change our minds.

But what if the only permission we need is our own?

A Soul-Level Stirring

One morning, journalling before my family woke, words spilled out before I could censor them:

"I want to speak on stage. I want to write a book. I want to coach others out of their stuck places."

I panicked. I snapped the journal shut like I'd written something forbidden.

Who did I think I was?

A nurse educator with a secure job, wanting to be a speaker?

A mother of three with stretch marks, dreaming of writing a book?

A burnt-out professional daring to coach others?

But the truth was undeniable: I didn't just want more—I was ready for it.

I wasn't ungrateful, I was awakening.

There's a difference between being content and being called.

- *Being content* says: *"This is enough."*
- *Being called* says: *"There's more, and it's waiting for you."*

That day, I stopped apologising for wanting more. I chose to explore what "more" could look like.

Strategy Spotlight: Granting Yourself Permission to Dream

- **Listen to Your Soul's Whispers** – Don't dismiss that quiet question: *"What if there's more?"* It's an invitation to growth.
- **Challenge the "Be Grateful" Trap** – Gratitude isn't meant to imprison you. You can be grateful *and* want more.
- **Name Your True Desires** – Write them down without censoring yourself. Clarity begins with honesty.
- **Create Your Own Permission Slip** – You don't need validation from anyone else. Give yourself written permission to change, grow, and dream.
- **Reimagine Success** – Align your goals with your purpose, not just your titles or achievements.

Reflection Questions

1. Have you silenced your dreams because they didn't seem "practical"?
2. What dreams did you have before life taught you to be "realistic"?
3. What would you pursue if you didn't need permission from anyone else?

Key Affirmation:

"I give myself full permission to dream, desire, and design a life that excites my soul." Motivationalee

The Pivot Point: Courage for the Change You Secretly Want

Key Takeaways

- Deferred dreams aren't denied—they're simply waiting for you to remember them.
- The first step to change is allowing yourself to want something different.
- You don't need validation to dream. You need vision.
- Wanting more isn't selfish—it's honest.

Action Steps

1. **Write Your Untold Dreams**

   Open a journal and list everything you've ever wanted to do, be or try. Don't filter—just dream.

2. **Speak It Aloud**

   Share one of those dreams with someone you trust. Saying it out loud makes it real.

3. **Create a Permission Slip**

   Write yourself a literal permission slip. Example:
   "I, [Your Name], give myself permission to explore becoming a speaker, author, coach..."
   Post it somewhere you'll see every day.

4. **Follow the Joy**

   Notice what excites you—even a little. Follow those sparks. They often lead to purpose.

5. **Find a Mentor or Model**

   Look for someone already doing what you dream of. Study their path. It's proof it's possible.

Lee Montajes

Part Two:
The Courage To Pivot

Chapter 9:
Daring to Want More

Original Quote:

"Your desire is not a disruption to your life—it's a divine invitation to rise."
— MotivationaLee

Desire Is Not a Dirty Word

For the longest time, I believed that wanting more meant I wasn't grateful.

After all, I had what many people dream of: a respected nursing career, a leadership role, a beautiful family, a roof over our heads. I had studied, sacrificed, and shown up again and again.

Who was I to want more?

But here's what no one tells you: gratitude and growth are not enemies.

You can be deeply grateful *and* still crave expansion. In fact, it's often gratitude that gives us the courage to rise—not stay small.

Still, I wrestled with it.

I remember journalling late one evening, after the kids had finally gone to sleep. The house was quiet. The scent of lavender swirled from my essential oil diffuser. I should've felt relaxed.

But something stirred in me.

I picked up my pen and wrote:

I want to speak on stage. I want to impact lives—not just lecture students. I want to coach people through the chaos I barely survived. I want to write a book. I want to become more than this role. I love nursing... but I know there's something more.

And then I cried.

Not out of sadness—but because I had finally spoken a truth I'd buried beneath responsibilities, routines and the expectations of everyone else.

That moment was not burnout from exhaustion.

It was burnout from misalignment.

A Bigger Life Calling

Desire doesn't appear in your heart by accident.

It's not noise. It's not distraction.

It's the whisper of your future calling you forward.

It's your soul tapping gently at the door, saying, *"There's more."*

But desire can be terrifying—especially for women like us.

We've been conditioned to dismiss it.

To be content.

To serve others first.

To not rock the boat.

To make our lives look "enough"—even when they no longer feel like they are.

So we build a life that checks every box… while slowly disconnecting from ourselves.

One day, I stood at the front of a classroom teaching about chronic stress and its effect on health. Mid-sentence, something clicked.

Here I am, educating others about stress… while living in a constant state of it myself.

I had become a messenger who wasn't living her own message.

That realisation hit hard. It wasn't a lack of knowledge. It wasn't a lack of skill.

It was a lack of **permission**—and I had been waiting for someone else to give it to me.

The Pivot Point: Courage for the Change You Secretly Want

Until I gave it to myself.

Sacred Discontent

Discontent is not failure. It's not a flaw. It's not ingratitude.

It's a sacred signal.

A gentle alarm clock from your soul.

It's the inner truth saying, *"This life no longer fits—not because it was wrong, but because you've grown."*

Like a seedling pushing against the edges of a pot, you've simply outgrown the container.

And you were never meant to stay confined.

I began experimenting with "more."

I spoke at small local events.

I offered free coaching sessions to practice.

I started a blog—five people read it (three of them were family).

But those baby steps weren't small to my soul.

They were *sacred*.

And with each step, I woke up the dreamer inside me.

Strategy Spotlight: Turning Desire Into Direction

- **Honour the Stirring** – When a desire persists, don't push it away. Explore what it might be pointing you toward.

- **Distinguish Desire from Distraction** – Ask: *Is this calling me toward alignment or just away from discomfort?*

- **Give Yourself Permission** – Don't wait for external approval. Write your own internal "permission slip" to want more.

- **Start Where You Are** – Growth doesn't require grand gestures. Begin with one action that moves you closer to your desire.

- **Redefine Ambition** – It's not selfish to want more. It's self-honouring when your growth creates impact.

Reflection Questions

1. Have you been taught to suppress your desires out of fear of being "too much"?
2. What would it look like to fully honour what you *really* want?
3. How can you tell the difference between a fleeting craving and a soul-level desire?

Key Affirmation:

"I allow myself to want more—and I trust that my desires are divine clues, not dangerous lies." Motivationalee

Key Takeaways

- Wanting more doesn't mean you're ungrateful—it means you're evolving.
- Discontent isn't the end of gratitude—it's the beginning of growth.
- Desire is the soul's map—it leads you back to your purpose.
- You are allowed to change. You are allowed to dream again.
- You don't need to justify your expansion. You just need to honour it.

Action Steps

1. **Name the Desire**

    Write a letter to yourself starting with "I want…" Let the words flow without editing.

2. **Trace the Origin**

    Ask yourself where the desire comes from—is it rooted in external approval or internal alignment?

3. **Give It Legitimacy**

    Share your desire with someone you trust. Practice saying, "This matters to me."

The Pivot Point: Courage for the Change You Secretly Want

4. **Start Small, Stay Steady**

    Take one small action this week—a conversation, a post, a course, or even research. Movement matters.

5. **Anchor in Truth**

Create a mantra that reminds you: *"My desires are divine, and I am safe to follow them."* Motivationalee

Chapter 10:
Letting Go of Titles, Holding On to Truth

Original Quote:

"You are not your title. You are not your résumé. You are not your job. You are the breath beneath all that—you are becoming."
MotivationaLee

For years, *Clinical Nurse Specialist* wasn't just a title—it was my identity.

It was how I introduced myself at conferences. How I justified my value. How I measured my worth.

It was also my shield.

Behind it, I could hide my fatigue. My frustration. My forgotten dreams.

People didn't ask how I was doing—they asked what I was doing. And because I was always *doing*, I stayed distracted from who I was *becoming*.

But identity built only on performance is like a house of cards. The moment life shakes the table, it all collapses.

And my table was starting to tremble.

The Inner Earthquake

I remember one morning after a brutal week of clinical shifts, coaching calls, parenting and university lectures.

I stood in front of the mirror and barely recognised the woman staring back.

Dark circles. Dull eyes. Forced smile.

My title still sounded impressive. But my truth felt hollow.

That day, I asked myself:

"Who am I... if I'm not Nurse Lee?"

The Pivot Point: Courage for the Change You Secretly Want

Not "Ma'am." Not "Educator." Not "Expert." Just… me.

The question terrified me.

Because I realised how much of my life had been about *proving* instead of *living*.

I was so busy earning significance that I lost sight of my soul's significance.

That moment cracked something open in me.

I began stripping away roles, expectations, accolades—asking myself:

"If no one was watching, what life would I choose?"

It wasn't easy.

We're taught to wear titles like armour:

- *The Strong One*
- *The Selfless One*
- *The High Achiever*
- *The One Who Has It All Together*

We wear them for safety. For approval. For belonging.

But they often bury our truth.

It's no wonder so many high-achieving women feel lost the moment they slow down.

When the performance stops, the panic starts.

Not because we're weak—but because we never built an identity rooted in *being*. Only in *doing*.

Letting go of a title doesn't mean dismissing your journey. It means refusing to hide behind it.

Your work is what you've *done*.

Your soul is who you *are*.

You were always more than your title.

Stripping It Back to Truth

The day I started introducing myself simply as *Lee* instead of *Nurse Educator*, something shifted.

People saw me. They heard my story. They connected with my *heart*, not just my credentials.

I learned this powerful truth:

People are drawn to your realness, not your résumé.

And when I began showing up as the woman beneath the title, new doors opened.

Not because I was proving anything.

But because I was finally living in alignment with truth.

I still love being a nurse. That calling will always be part of my story.

But now I see it as a chapter—not the whole book.

Strategy Spotlight: Releasing Titles to Reclaim Self

- **Notice Your Masks** – Pay attention to roles you use to feel safe or valuable. Ask yourself: *Is this who I am, or what I do?*
- **Practice Introducing Your Essence** – Try sharing your passions or purpose instead of your job title.
- **Allow Yourself to Be Seen** – Let people meet the real you—flawed, growing, authentic.
- **Redefine Worth** – Remember that your value doesn't depend on performance. You are worthy because you *are*.
- **Make Space for Becoming** – Schedule time to simply *be*. No tasks. No goals. Just you.

Reflection Questions

1. What titles, roles or labels have you tied your identity to?
2. If all of those were stripped away, what would remain?

The Pivot Point: Courage for the Change You Secretly Want

3. What version of you is waiting to emerge once you stop performing?

Key Affirmation:

"I am not defined by my title—I am defined by my truth. And my truth is powerful." Motivationalee

Key Takeaways

- Titles are useful, but they are not your true identity.
- Performing for approval can lead to internal disconnection.
- Releasing titles creates space for deeper alignment and authenticity.
- You are worthy simply by being, not just by doing.

Action Steps

1. **Journal the Question**

   Write a response to: *Who am I without my title?* Let it flow freely, without judgement.

2. **Audit Your Attachments**

   List the titles and roles you carry. Which feel authentic? Which feel like performance?

3. **Practice Being, Not Doing**

   Set aside 15 minutes daily with no tasks or goals. Just be. Notice what emerges.

4. **Speak From the Soul**

   Introduce yourself at least once this week without using your job title. Try: *"Hi, I'm [Name], and I'm passionate about [truth]."*

5. **Affirm Your Essence**

   Say aloud: *"My worth is not tied to any role. I am enough, exactly as I am."*

Chapter 11: The Day I Chose Me

"One day you'll stop abandoning yourself to keep the peace—and that will be the beginning of your freedom."
MotivationaLee

For most of my life, I was a *giver*.

I wore that identity like a badge of honour.

I gave in the hospital.

I gave in the classroom.

I gave at home.

I gave in conversations, in church, in relationships, in boardrooms.

I gave and gave… until I disappeared under the weight of what I thought was love and loyalty.

They called it *dedication*.

They called it *excellence*.

They called it *service*.

But inside, I was drowning in a silent scream:

When is it my turn?

And then—one day—I made a decision.

A decision that felt selfish.

A decision that felt rebellious.

A decision that felt scary.

But also… sacred.

That was the day I chose me.

The Pivot Point: Courage for the Change You Secretly Want

The Moment It Shifted

It wasn't dramatic. There was no big announcement. No social media post.

Just a quiet moment in the car outside the hospital after another 14-hour shift.

I was supposed to walk into a leadership meeting. I had skipped dinner. My phone had 12 unread messages. I was needed. Again.

But as I sat there, hands on the steering wheel, heart pounding with fatigue, I whispered:

"I can't keep doing this."

And it wasn't the *I'm just tired* kind of can't.

This was soul-deep.

This was unsustainable.

In that silence, a thought came:

"What if you didn't go in? What if, just this once, you chose your peace over your duty?"

It wasn't a breakdown.

It was a breakthrough.

I started the car—and drove home.

I said no to something I would have once forced myself to say yes to.

And though guilt rose in my throat like fire, I also felt something I hadn't felt in years:

Relief.

When Self-Sacrifice Becomes Self-Abandonment

Let's be clear: *service* is beautiful. *Giving* is honourable.

But there's a difference between serving from fullness and serving from depletion.

For years, I mistook people-pleasing for kindness. I confused overworking with worthiness. I believed choosing myself meant betraying others.

But I know the truth now:

Every time I said yes to what drained me, I was saying no to what could free me.

Self-abandonment doesn't always look like despair.

Sometimes it looks like hyper-productivity.

Perfectionism.

Smiling while silently suffocating.

And slowly, we disappear.

Choosing You Is Not a Betrayal—It's a Breakthrough

That day in the car was the first domino.

One brave "no" led to another.

I said no to staying late when my kids needed me more.

I said no to opportunities that paid well but cost me my peace.

I said no to toxic dynamics that fed on my silence.

But every "no" was really a "yes":

- Yes, to healing.
- Yes, to rest.
- Yes, to alignment.
- Yes, to my truth.

Choosing yourself doesn't mean abandoning your responsibilities.

It means showing up for them without abandoning your soul.

I learned the world won't fall apart if you rest.

But you might fall apart if you don't.

The Pivot Point: Courage for the Change You Secretly Want

The Woman I'm Becoming

Every time I chose myself, I discovered a new version of me.

Stronger.

Softer.

Sharper.

Not hard from burnout, but resilient from boundaries.

Not selfish, but self-aware.

Not cold, but no longer co-dependent.

And the more I honoured her—the woman I was becoming—the less I craved external validation.

I didn't need everyone to agree.

I needed me to be free.

That was the day my pivot truly began.

Strategy Spotlight: Moving from Self-Abandonment to Self-Honouring

- **Recognise the Signs** – Notice when you're saying yes out of fear, guilt, or obligation rather than genuine desire.
- **Normalise Saying No** – Remember that "no" is a complete sentence. It doesn't require endless explanation.
- **Redefine Responsibility** – Serving well doesn't mean sacrificing yourself. True responsibility includes caring for your own wellbeing.
- **Choose Small Acts of Self-Loyalty** – Start with one boundary today, no matter how small.
- **Honour the Guilt as Growth** – Guilt isn't a sign you're wrong. It's often a sign you're doing something new—and necessary.

Reflection Questions

1. When was the last time you abandoned yourself to keep the peace?
2. What warning signs tell you you're betraying your own needs?
3. What does choosing yourself look like in this season of your life?

Key Affirmation:

"Choosing myself is not selfish—it's sacred. I deserve to live, not just survive." Motivationalee

Key Takeaways

- Choosing yourself often begins in quiet moments of truth.
- People-pleasing is not the same as genuine service.
- Saying "no" to what drains you is saying "yes" to alignment.
- The pivot begins the moment you choose your truth over obligation.

Action Steps

1. **Identify a Pattern**

    List three situations where you consistently abandon your needs. Ask yourself: *Is this love or fear?*

2. **Set One Boundary**

    Choose one area (work, family, friendship) where you will set a gentle but firm boundary. Practise saying: *"Not right now. I need to take care of myself."*

3. **Create a "Yes to Me" List**

    Write down ten things you'd do if you weren't afraid of disappointing others. Choose one and do it this week.

4. **Rest Without Earning It**

    Schedule rest—not as a reward, but as a right. Take 30 minutes this week to do nothing and notice how your body feels.

The Pivot Point: Courage for the Change You Secretly Want

5. **Affirm It Daily**

    Say aloud each morning: *"Today, I choose me—and that choice creates space for others to do the same." Motivationalee*

Chapter 12: Rebuilding From the Inside Out

Original Quote:

"You don't need to rebuild your life the way it was. You're not who you were."
MotivationaLee

There comes a moment, after the breaking and the choosing, when you're left staring at the rubble of what used to be your life.

The titles are laid down.

The roles are paused.

The expectations have cracked open.

And what remains… is you.

Not the version they trained, titled, or celebrated—

but the version that trembles with truth.

This is where real rebuilding begins.

Not with a five-year plan.

Not with a career switch.

But with the slow, sacred work of *becoming*.

Life After the Storm

After that pivotal day I chose myself, there wasn't immediate clarity.

People talk about breakthroughs like they're magic moments that fix everything.

But they don't tell you about the mess that follows.

I felt lost.

Like I'd burned the map but had no compass.

I was still a nurse.

The Pivot Point: Courage for the Change You Secretly Want

Still a mother.

Still a leader in many ways.

But something had shifted.

I no longer wanted to perform. I wanted to *live*.

But what does living look like when you've been surviving for so long?

That question led me on a journey that demanded more courage than any hospital emergency, more strength than any double shift.

It asked me to rebuild my identity—not on what I did, but on who I *truly* was.

The Internal Renovation

Rebuilding from the inside out meant unlearning everything I was taught made me valuable:

- Productivity
- Perfection
- Performance
- Pleasing people

It meant:

- Healing wounds I'd ignored for years
- Sitting in silence and facing my inner critic
- Learning to be kind to the woman in the mirror

I had to deconstruct my worth from my work.

I had to let go of the belief that being "strong" meant never asking for help.

I had to forgive myself for staying too long in places that didn't honour me.

This wasn't self-improvement.

This was *soul excavation*.

One journal entry at a time.

One therapy session at a time.

One tearful prayer at a time.

I rebuilt.

Not a new job.

A new foundation.

The Power of Rebuilding Slowly

The world says *rise quickly*.

I chose to rise *intentionally*.

I didn't leap into the next big thing.

I slowed down.

I spent more time with my children—not just being there, but truly *present*.

I started writing again.

Coaching.

Speaking.

Teaching from the *heart*, not from a script.

For the first time, I felt *free*.

Because I wasn't chasing.

I was *creating*.

Rebuilding isn't about returning to normal.

It's about redefining what *whole* looks like for you.

The Woman Emerging

Each day I rebuilt, a different woman began to surface.

She didn't care so much about applause.

The Pivot Point: Courage for the Change You Secretly Want

She didn't shrink to make others comfortable.

She didn't beg to be seen—she *stood*.

She was me.

The real me.

The one I buried under burnout and busyness.

The one I abandoned to meet everyone else's needs.

She came back.

Not perfectly.

Not loudly.

But *powerfully*.

And I made her a promise:

Never again will I build a life that costs me myself.

Strategy Spotlight: Rebuilding from the Inside Out

- **Honour the Rubble** – Don't rush past what fell apart. Sit with it. Learn from it.
- **Define Your Values** – Choose values that will guide your new life—peace, freedom, creativity, connection.
- **Slow the Pace** – Resist the urge to "fix" everything immediately. Rebuilding slowly creates depth and sustainability.
- **Create from Alignment** – Don't chase the next thing for approval. Build what feels true and aligned.
- **Forgive the Past You** – Let go of guilt for staying too long in old patterns. She did her best with what she knew.

Reflection Questions

1. What version of you has been buried under your current roles?
2. What old beliefs no longer serve this new season?

3. How would your life look if it was built around peace instead of pressure?

Key Affirmation:

"I am rebuilding not what I had—but what I truly need. This time, I choose wholeness over hustle." Motivationalee

Key Takeaways

- Rebuilding begins after you've let go—not before.
- Your identity is not your productivity.
- Healing is the foundation of sustainable success.
- Rebuilding slowly creates something sacred, not shallow.

Action Steps

1. **Journal the Rubble**

   Write down everything that crumbled in your old life—expectations, patterns, beliefs. What are you grateful to leave behind?

2. **List Your Core Values**

   Identify 3–5 values that will define your new life (e.g. peace, freedom, creativity, connection). Let them guide your decisions.

3. **Create a Wholeness Routine**

   Build a weekly habit that nurtures your inner world (therapy, quiet time, nature walks, coaching, etc.).

4. **Declutter Your Calendar**

   Remove one commitment this month that doesn't align with your peace or purpose. Say yes only to what supports the life you're rebuilding.

5. **Celebrate Small Progress**

   Rebuilding isn't glamorous. Acknowledge each small shift you make—these are the bricks that build your future.

Chapter 13:
Critics, Comparisons, and Courage

Original Quote:

"The volume of your critics and the highlight reel of others can drown out your own calling—unless you decide your voice matters more."
MotivationaLee

When you decide to pivot—whether it's leaving a job, changing careers, stepping back from people-pleasing, or finally choosing yourself—there will be *noise*.

Not from your intuition.

But from *them*.

The critics.

The onlookers.

The voices that never fully supported you but still feel entitled to narrate your story.

And as if their judgment wasn't enough, you also start scrolling through the curated, filtered highlights of everyone else's life.

While you're rebuilding from the ground up, it can seem like others are soaring effortlessly.

You start to wonder:

"Am I too late?"

"Am I even doing the right thing?"

"Who do I think I am to try something new?"

This chapter is about reclaiming your power in a world that profits from your self-doubt.

The Critics That Live Rent-Free

The first critic I had to confront wasn't on social media or in my workplace.

It lived in my own head.

It whispered:

- *"You're being selfish."*
- *"People will think you've failed."*
- *"Who do you think you are to dream this big?"*

These weren't new voices.

They were old recordings—echoes of perfectionism, cultural pressure, self-protection.

They reflected years of needing to prove myself in high-performance environments.

But this time, I chose not to listen.

Because here's what I realised:

Critics don't pay your bills, live your life, or carry the cost of your burnout.

So why should they direct your next chapter?

Comparison: The Silent Thief

One morning, during a particularly vulnerable season of rebuilding, I opened social media and saw someone I used to work with celebrating a new executive role.

She looked radiant. Successful. Glowing.

And there I was—working part-time, still figuring things out, coaching a handful of people, wondering if I'd made a mistake.

Comparison hit me like a gut punch.

I had to remind myself:

The Pivot Point: Courage for the Change You Secretly Want

Her lane is not mine.

Her race is not mine.

Her reward is not mine.

Comparison shrinks your courage.

It convinces you to delay your destiny because someone else is moving faster or shinier.

But I was no longer in a race.

I was in a *realignment*.

And that requires a different kind of strength.

Cultivating Courage in the Face of Judgment

Courage doesn't mean you don't care what people think.

It means you care more about *becoming who you were born to be* than about being liked by everyone along the way.

I've been judged for leaving a stable job.

Questioned for choosing speaking over certainty.

Criticised for sharing too openly about grief, burnout, and rebirth.

I've felt it—that bitter silence in the room when I succeeded.

The ones who said, *"I'm happy for you,"* but never clapped.

The ones who wore masks of support, only to watch closely—hoping I'd fail.

Some people weren't cheering.

They were competing.

They envied the courage I had that they couldn't summon.

They saw my pivot as a threat, not an inspiration.

They mistook my purpose for pride, when all I wanted was peace.

There are people in this world—maybe even close to you—

who are just waiting for you to fail.

But hear this:

What they say does not define your success.

Your calling isn't up for public vote.

And your courage will always be louder than their envy, if you let it speak.

I had to stop shrinking to make others comfortable.

My success didn't require their applause.

My purpose didn't need their permission.

Because at the end of the day, *your destiny will not be delayed by their disbelief.*

You just need to be *authentic.*

Letting Go of the Need to Be Liked

People-pleasing was a deep-rooted habit I had to unlearn.

It served me well in fast-paced, high-pressure environments.

It helped me avoid conflict, gain approval, stay "safe."

But people-pleasing will keep you imprisoned in a life that no longer fits.

So I began practising tiny rebellions:

- Saying no without explaining myself
- Sharing vulnerably online even when it felt scary
- Setting boundaries even if others felt disappointed

Each small act was a vote for my freedom.

And slowly, I became someone who didn't just talk about courage—

I *embodied* it.

The Pivot Point: Courage for the Change You Secretly Want

Words That Freed Me

Here are a few truths I held onto whenever criticism or comparison tried to derail me:

- *"Their opinion is not my obligation."*
- *"I don't need to be understood to be aligned."*

"My story is still unfolding—and that's okay."

Sometimes courage isn't loud.

Sometimes it's a quiet decision to keep going—even when no one claps.

Strategy Spotlight: Staying True in a World That Doubts You

- **Name the Critics** – Identify who or what voices are influencing your decisions. Are they aligned with your growth?
- **Rewrite the Narrative** – Challenge old beliefs that say you're selfish or foolish for changing.
- **Choose Your Pace** – Your journey isn't a race. Honour the slow, intentional steps.
- **Curate Your Inputs** – Clean up your social feeds, conversations, and spaces to reflect your values and goals.
- **Celebrate Your Rebellions** – Notice and honour each moment you choose authenticity over approval.

Reflection Questions

1. Who are the critics (internal or external) influencing your choices right now?
2. What part of your story do you feel tempted to hide because of fear of judgment?
3. How can you support yourself when comparison starts to cloud your vision?

Key Affirmation:

"I am not here to impress the world—I'm here to become the woman I was always meant to be." Motivationalee

Key Takeaways

- Your pivot will stir opinions—but their noise doesn't cancel your clarity.
- Comparison only works if you forget your unique path.
- Courage means showing up even when you feel uncertain or unseen.
- The need to be liked can delay the life you're meant to live.

Action Steps

1. **Name the Critics**

   Write down specific voices (real or imagined) creating fear or doubt in your transition. Identify the core message they're sending.

2. **Create a Courage Script**

   Replace each negative belief with a truth. For example, *"They'll think I'm lost"* becomes *"I'm not lost, I'm aligning."*

3. **Detox Your Social Feed**

   Unfollow or mute accounts that trigger comparison. Curate your digital space to reflect your values and pace.

4. **Take a Bold Action**

   Post that message. Have that conversation. Apply for that opportunity. Do one thing that would terrify your inner critic and free your truest self.

5. **Celebrate Your Bravery**

   Keep a "Courage Journal" to record each brave step you take. This is your personal record of strength.

Part Three:
The Birth of a New Purpose

Chapter 14:
From Nurse to Coach — A Story of Alignment

Original Quote:

> *"When purpose whispers louder than fear, the pivot becomes inevitable."*
> *MotivationaLee*

There comes a moment in every journey when the dots begin to connect—not backwards, as Steve Jobs once said, but inward.

This chapter isn't about burnout. It's about breakthrough. It's not about running away from something, but running toward something that had been quietly waiting for me all along.

I didn't leave nursing because I stopped loving it. I left because something else began calling to me more deeply.

It didn't happen overnight. Coaching found me in whispers—first through late-night conversations with colleagues who sought more than clinical advice, and then through students I mentored who thanked me for seeing their potential, not just correcting their charts.

I began to realise: I wasn't just good at nursing. I was called to guide, to speak life, and to help others reconnect with the parts of themselves they had long silenced.

One day, in the stillness of my morning devotion, the truth rose like the sun:

You were meant to help others heal beyond the body.

That was the pivot.

That was the moment of alignment.

For years, my life was framed by the sounds of beeping monitors, sterile white walls, and the steady rhythm of the hospital floor. I wore my title like armour— Senior Nurse, Theatre Team Lead, Clinical

The Pivot Point: Courage for the Change You Secretly Want

Educator, Nurse educator, Learning Facilitator (Bachelor and Diploma of Nursing). It gave me credibility, responsibility, and a sense of identity.

But slowly—almost imperceptibly—the very things that once defined me began to feel like chains.

The pivot didn't come overnight. It never does.

It began in moments—quiet, sacred, sometimes painful.

Moments when I stood in front of my nursing students and felt more alive speaking life into their careers than I had in months on the hospital floor. Moments when I looked beyond the charts and started asking deeper questions about healing—not just of the body, but of the heart and soul.

I had survived burnout, personal collapse, and a terrifying brush with physical shutdown. I shared part of that in Chapter 4.

But Chapter 12 is not about the breaking.

It's about the building.

The Pull of a New Calling

What started as mentoring new graduates soon turned into informal life coaching.

One student would stay after class to talk. Then another. Then a colleague asked if I could help her navigate a career transition.

It was never part of my "job description," but it always felt like part of my destiny.

People began to say:

"You should be a coach."

"You speak with such clarity and wisdom."

"You helped me see what I couldn't."

For a while, I resisted the idea.

How could I just leave nursing? Wouldn't that mean abandoning all the years, the sweat, the sacrifices?

But the truth was, I wasn't abandoning anything—I was building on it.

Teaching. Mentoring. Coaching. Speaking. Writing.

They weren't detours from my nursing career.

They were **expansions** of it.

Extensions of the same heartbeat that led me to care for people in the first place.

The Sacred Bridge Between Two Callings

Coaching didn't compete with my nursing experience—it completed it.

Everything I had learned as a nurse—the empathy, the quick decision-making, the heart for people—became the foundation of my coaching style.

My intuition was sharper.

My emotional intelligence, honed in trauma rooms and tender moments, became my greatest coaching asset.

This pivot wasn't just a career shift.

It was a soul shift.

I went from healing wounds to healing identities.

From checking vitals to reviving visions.

From helping others survive… to helping them thrive.

And the deeper I leaned into it, the more fulfilled I became.

The Power of Saying Yes to Alignment

Alignment doesn't shout. It whispers.

It's the inner peace that rises when you do what you were born to do.

The Pivot Point: Courage for the Change You Secretly Want

When I began coaching officially—not just on the side, but as my new vocation—something shifted in my energy, my language, and my joy.

People noticed.

"You're glowing," someone said after a workshop.

"No, I'm just… aligned," I smiled.

That alignment wasn't just internal—it transformed my family life.

I had more time with my children.

More present conversations with my husband.

More energy to pursue projects that made my heart race—in the best way.

My calendar still had appointments.

But now, they were filled with **purpose**.

Strategy Spotlight: Embracing the Pivot with Purpose

- **Listen for the Whispers** – Pay attention to the subtle nudges, moments of joy, and recurring inner prompts calling you toward something more.
- **Reframe the Shift** – Don't see change as abandoning your past; view it as building on everything you've already become.
- **Identify the Transferable** – List the skills, experiences, and values from your previous role that now serve your new purpose.
- **Normalise the Tension** – It's okay to feel both fear and excitement—both are signs you're stepping into something meaningful.
- **Act Before You're "Ready"** – Clarity comes through movement. Take one aligned action, even if it feels small or uncertain.

Reflection Questions

- What parts of your current life feel aligned with your purpose? What feels out of alignment?
- Have you ever ignored a whisper from within because it didn't fit the expectations others had for you?
- What gift or skill have people always come to you for—even when you didn't charge for it?

Key Affirmation:

"I trust the whispers of alignment. I have permission to pivot into the life I was created to live." Motivationalee

Key Takeaways

- Alignment often starts as a whisper before it becomes a roar.
- Your past profession may prepare you for your next purpose—it's not wasted.
- Clarity comes through action, not just thought. Start, even if it's small.

Action Steps

1. Write down three things that light you up—activities where time flies when you're doing them.
2. Ask five trusted people what strengths or gifts they see in you—there's often a pattern.
3. Choose one aligned action to take this week toward a new purpose: sign up for a course, create a workshop outline, or speak your dream aloud.

Chapter 15:
From Grief to Grace —
The Legacy of My Father

Original Quote:

"When you are a laborer, your life evolves around your work. But when you're an entrepreneur, your work evolves around your life."
My Father, Antonio Paner Perez

There are moments in life when everything seems to fall into place — your career, your plans, your dreams.

In 2016, I was living that moment.

I had moved to Melbourne and was working part-time as a Clinical Nurse Educator. The shift from full-time clinical nursing to teaching and training felt like a breath of fresh air — a transition I had longed for.

Between classroom lectures and clinical placements, I was thriving. I was delivering workshops, seeing my vision take shape, and finally feeling aligned. It felt as though all my years of hard work were creating space for the woman I was becoming.

But even in that beautiful season, there was a quiet longing in my soul — a whisper I couldn't ignore.

Yes, I loved teaching. Yes, I was good at it. My students, colleagues, and friends would often say, *"You've got nothing more to prove. You're a brilliant nurse. A gifted educator."*

But deep down, I wasn't asking if I was good at what I did.

I was asking: *What else was I born to do?*

The Restlessness Behind the Success

Since the 1990s, I had carried a quiet passion for coaching. I knew I had a gift for inspiring and guiding others, but the idea of turning that into a career felt too risky.

Becoming an entrepreneur meant leaving behind the safety of a stable income — and potentially, a piece of my identity.

Still, something had begun to stir inside me.

I found myself drawn to the words of Tony Robbins and Simon Sinek. Their questions pierced my heart — especially one I couldn't answer clearly:

What is your why?

Despite the outward success, I was overworked, underpaid, and emotionally depleted.

Tears became part of my daily routine.

I wasn't thriving.

I was surviving.

And though I could feel the pull toward something more, I had no idea how to bridge the gap between where I was and where I longed to be.

Then the Call Came

In the midst of this search for clarity, life collapsed in a single phone call:

My father, Antonio Paner Perez, had suffered a massive stroke overseas.

I was devastated.

I flew home to the Philippines and spent five precious weeks at his bedside in the ICU. Five weeks watching the strongest man I knew lie still and fragile, slipping away.

I wanted to stay longer, but responsibilities in Melbourne called. I had workshops to deliver. Bills to pay. I was the only child — the breadwinner. And the pressure weighed heavily.

I returned to Australia carrying a heavy heart, using work to distract myself. But I didn't realise I was sprinting straight into another storm.

The Pivot Point: Courage for the Change You Secretly Want

Only weeks later, while still drowning in catch-up and chaos, the call came again:

My father was gone.

The grief shattered me. I felt guilt. I felt failure. I felt like I had betrayed the very reason I became a nurse — to care for others, especially those I loved.

The Final Gift of a Father

When I returned for his funeral, I stood before his coffin trembling. I felt the weight of our history, my responsibilities, and the dreams I had put on hold.

Then, in the silence of that moment, something profound happened.

His voice echoed in my mind — clear, calm, and certain:

"You will never feel more successful, secure, or content staying a labourer for life than you will becoming an entrepreneur. As a labourer, your life evolves around your work. But as an entrepreneur, your work evolves with your life."

His words broke through my grief like sunlight through storm clouds.

This was the same man who had taught me discipline, sacrifice, and humility — now giving me permission. A divine nudge to step fully into my calling. A final gift from the man who gave me life, now urging me to live it.

That moment was my **mindshift**.

I realised then that my fear of coaching, of speaking, of becoming an entrepreneur — wasn't a flaw. It was a threshold.

And my father's legacy demanded I cross it.

Strategy Spotlight: Transforming Loss Into Legacy

- **Let Grief Speak** – In moments of deep loss, listen closely. Grief often carries clarity that logic alone cannot offer.

- **Honour the Inner Shift** – When life breaks you open, don't rush to rebuild. Pause. There may be a new path waiting to emerge.
- **Redefine Security** – True stability isn't in paychecks or titles. It's in living a life that aligns with your truth.
- **Turn Their Words into Fuel** – What wisdom did your loved one leave behind? Let it guide your next steps.
- **Make the Legacy Active** – Don't just remember them — represent them. Let their influence live through the boldness of your choices.

Reflection Questions
- What moment in your life cracked you open to a deeper truth?
- Is there a message from someone you've lost that still guides you today?
- What legacy do you feel responsible to carry forward?

Key Affirmation:

"I honour the legacy of those who came before me by becoming all I was born to be. My pain has a purpose. I carry their light forward through my courage." Motivationalee

Key Takeaways
- Grief can become a doorway to purpose, if you let it teach you.
- Clarity often comes through pain — not in spite of it.
- Our dreams don't die with those we lose — sometimes, they awaken because of them.

Action Steps
1. **Write your "mindshift" moment** — capture the moment pain revealed a new purpose.
2. **Reflect on someone you've lost.** What lessons from them still shape your life?

The Pivot Point: Courage for the Change You Secretly Want

3. **Set a new goal in their honour.** Let it be the next brave step you take.

4. **Say their name. Share their wisdom.** Keeping their voice alive keeps their legacy alive.

5. **Use your pain as a platform.** Let your story be a light for someone else navigating the dark.

Chapter 16:
The Unexpected Birth That Changed Everything

Original Quote:

"There are moments when time stands still — not because the world paused, but because your soul just met its purpose."
MotivationaLee

Thirteen years after giving birth to my first child, I found myself standing at a surprising crossroads: I was pregnant again — at 43.

The year was 2018. I was still swimming through waves of grief after losing my father in 2017. His death had cracked something deep inside me, and I was slowly trying to rebuild myself — emotionally, mentally, and spiritually.

Then life offered me something unexpected.

A new heartbeat.

A tiny, sacred whisper from within.

A daughter.

A miracle.

A calling.

It felt like a divine exchange had taken place.

I lost my father — the man who taught me strength, leadership, and vision.

And I gained a daughter — a new soul entrusted to me, full of light and possibility.

What does this mean?

In the quiet stillness of reflection, I came to believe this:

Where loss creates a void, love returns with purpose.

The Pivot Point: Courage for the Change You Secretly Want

I believe Lauren was sent to soften the loss and strengthen my legacy. Where my father's story ended, hers began — and somewhere in between, I was rewritten.

High Risk, But Fully Ready

Although doctors labelled me as high-risk due to my age, I felt strong. I felt ready. I was active, healthy, and deeply grateful for the gift of carrying life again — a miracle in itself.

But what happened next would become the pivot point of all pivot points.

A moment that hung literally between life and death.

A moment where everything — my motherhood, my purpose, my future — was surrendered at the feet of a God I fully trusted, even in the scariest silence.

The Hemorrhage: Where Life Hung by a Thread

The delivery began normally. I gave birth to Lauren naturally and held her for a brief, magical moment. But after the placenta was delivered, something shifted — fast.

A sudden whoosh. A strange heaviness.

Then blood. Lots of it.

I had lost over a third of my blood volume — a life-threatening postpartum haemorrhage. I was bleeding out, rapidly.

Code Blue. The room erupted in motion.

I could hear shouting — midwives, doctors, the MET team, nurses. The air was thick with panic, and yet, oddly, I felt calm. As if part of me had already accepted what was happening.

"Lee, stay with us! Keep breathing. We're here. Just stay awake."

But I was fading. The world dimmed. My body betrayed me, growing weaker. I was conscious, but slipping into a stillness that felt like the edge of goodbye.

As they prepared to rush me into emergency surgery, I whispered a surrender that would change my life forever:

"Lord, if this is the end, take care of my family. Let Your will be done. But... if You let me stay, I promise I'll live fully. I'll stop hiding. I'll use every gift You've given me — to speak, to coach, to write, to impact lives. No more fear. No more delay. Just purpose."

They wheeled me into theatre, and all I could do was sing.

Literally, sing.

Worship songs: "Lord I Offer My Life to You," and "Mighty to Save."

I didn't pray for survival — I prayed for alignment. For God's will.

I didn't fear death. In fact, I whispered:

"If I die, at least I'll see my Dad in heaven."

But if I lived... I would live boldly.

Then blackness.

The Awakening: Reborn into Purpose

When I woke up, I was groggy, wrapped in tubes, pain, and the soft voices of care. The surgery had been successful — just in time. I had survived a massive haemorrhage.

Consultants and nurses visited me. One said they heard me praying in tongues. Another said they felt goosebumps in the room.

I told them I was just singing worship songs — but maybe, just maybe, heaven sang with me.

And that's when everything changed.

I had been given another chance — not just to live, but to truly live.

I could have died, but I didn't.

I could have let that be a trauma that paralysed me. Instead, it became the birth not just of a daughter — but of a destiny.

That was the moment I pivoted from just being a nurse to being a

The Pivot Point: Courage for the Change You Secretly Want

vessel.

From working to survive, to working with meaning.

From pouring out, to finally pouring from overflow.

The Shift Toward Purpose

I began shifting my focus slowly — to classroom teaching, to mentoring, to coaching professional MC'ing, moderating and public speaking.

A life more balanced.

A calling more aligned.

That day redefined everything.

I finally understood why exhaustion had chased me into hospital toilets, why my body had broken down after 20-hour surgeries.

I had been pouring from an empty cup.

Saying yes to the world's expectations, while saying no to the whisper of my soul.

But not anymore.

Seven years later, I'm living proof of divine redirection.

I coach, I speak, I write, I host, I create — all with joy, all with ease, all with the fire of purpose.

God didn't just save my life.

He repurposed it.

And that, my friend, is the real birth story.

Strategy Spotlight: Living from Overflow

- **Name the Turning Point** – Identify the moment that changed everything. Name it. Own it. Let it become your anchor.
- **Rebuild with Intention** – Don't rush to return to "normal." Rebuild your life with sacred purpose and clarity.

- **Live Your Vow** – What you promised yourself in crisis is your soul's truth. Start living it — today.
- **Stop Pouring from Empty** – Purpose doesn't require burnout. Build systems, support, and rituals that protect your energy.
- **Create from Overflow** – Use your gifts not from obligation, but from abundance. That's where true impact lives.

Reflection Questions

- Have you ever experienced a moment where your life hung in the balance? What did it reveal to you?
- What vow have you made to yourself or to God in a moment of crisis — and are you living it?
- Are you surviving… or living with purpose?

Key Affirmation:

"I am capable, I am resilient, and I trust myself to handle whatever comes my way." Motivationlee

Key Takeaways

- Life's most painful moments can be the very catalyst for your greatest transformation.
- Surrendering to purpose often begins at the edge of yourself — when all you have left is faith.
- When life gives you another chance, don't waste it living small. Say yes. Say now.

Action Steps

1. **Write your surrender story** — What would you say if you were granted one more day, one more chance? Write it now — and then live it.
2. **Declare your pivot point** — Choose the moment that changed you forever, and name it. That's your turning point. Own it.
3. **Live your vow** — If you've promised yourself that you'll stop hiding your light, start living that promise today.
4. **Build from purpose** — List every gift you have — then find a way to use it for others. That's the fastest path to alignment.

The Pivot Point: Courage for the Change You Secretly Want

5. **Worship through the chaos** — Whether through music, prayer, or stillness — find a sacred ritual that carries you through life's storms.

Chapter 17: What My Daughters Taught Me About Purpose

Original Quote:

"Sometimes, the most profound life lessons are not taught in lecture halls or learned through years of experience—they're whispered in bedtime stories, spilled in car rides, and found in the simple, sacred chaos of raising daughters."
MotivationaLee

I became a mother three times. Each time, a different version of me was born too.

First came Izzy, my eldest, bright-eyed and full of questions. Then just sixteen months later came Yumi, with a quiet strength that grounded me. And thirteen years after that—when I least expected it—Lauren arrived, a miracle and a message from above.

Each daughter came in a different season of my life, and with them came new lessons, fresh awakenings, and a deeper understanding of what it really means to live on purpose.

When Izzy and Yumi were little, I was deep in my nursing career—working in the Operating Room, taking on critical care shifts, often on call with unpredictable hours. The shifts were intense. I would go from life-saving surgeries straight to rushing home, hoping not to miss another precious moment of their childhoods. But sometimes, I did.

Juggling Purpose and Profession

With rotating rosters, night shifts, and weekend calls, I missed some of their school milestones and events. I tried so hard to be there—but the tug-of-war between service at the hospital and presence at home was real. There were many days I was torn, heart aching, as I put on my scrubs instead of showing up at their school assembly.

Still, I made the moments count.

The Pivot Point: Courage for the Change You Secretly Want

I caught up on bedtime stories whenever I could, even when I was bone-tired. I'd pray with them in the car during school drop-offs, sometimes after an exhausting on-call night. I tucked love into every in-between space—between surgeries, between shifts, between exhaustion and determination.

I thought I was building a life for them, but in truth, they were shaping me.

Purpose, Reimagined

By the time Lauren came along thirteen years later, I was in a very different place—more spiritually grounded, more self-aware, and more open to surrender. Her birth, which nearly claimed my life, wasn't just dramatic. It was transformative.

Lauren's arrival felt like a divine interruption. She reminded me that life is sacred—not only in the operating theatre, but also in the quiet 2 a.m. feedings, the lullabies, and the messy moments that aren't productive but are profoundly powerful.

I began to understand that purpose isn't always tied to career or achievements. Sometimes, it's found on the floor playing with blocks. Sometimes, it's hidden in the whispered "I love yous" between dishes and deadlines. Sometimes, it's in the soft strength of simply being present.

My daughters taught me that being there matters more than doing it all.

They reminded me I am more than my roles. I am a woman of deep love, fierce loyalty, and a capacity to pivot—even when it's hard.

They gave me my "why."

Presence Over Perfection

In Izzy's creative spirit, Yumi's emotional depth, and Lauren's wild joy, I saw reflections of myself—and lessons I needed to learn.

When Izzy said, "Mum, I love when you're just you, not the busy you," I heard it loud and clear. That was all she ever wanted. Not perfection—just presence.

I realised that being a present mother was part of my calling, not separate from it.

One evening, after another long shift, I came home and found Yumi quietly colouring at the dining table. I sat beside her, exhausted but wanting to connect. Without looking up, she said softly, "Mum, you're always busy... but I know you love us because you always come back."

That one sentence stopped me in my tracks. Yumi, with her gentle soul and wisdom beyond her years, reminded me that presence isn't about quantity—it's about the quality of love felt in the moments we *do* have.

I began to integrate, not compartmentalise.

I allowed my girls to see the journey—not just the polished parts, but the messy middles, the tears, the pivots, and the rising.

My daughters taught me that legacy isn't about what I leave behind—it's about what I pour into them now.

Strategy Spotlight: Redefining Purpose Through Presence

- **Notice the Signals** – What are your loved ones subtly telling you about what they need from you?
- **Build Micro-Moments** – Don't wait for big events. Infuse purpose into daily routines like school runs, bedtime, or breakfast chats.
- **Shift the Scorecard** – Let go of traditional markers of success. Honour the quiet, powerful act of simply being there.

Reflection Questions

- How have your children or loved ones shaped your understanding of purpose?
- Are you trying to be everything to everyone—or are you allowing yourself to be present where it matters most?
- What small rituals or connections can you build with your loved ones today?

The Pivot Point: Courage for the Change You Secretly Want

Key Affirmation:

"I learn from those I love. I lead with presence. I am enough, even in stillness." Motivationalee

Action Steps

1. **Create Presence Rituals** – Choose one time in your day to connect intentionally with your child or loved one (e.g., bedtime talk, 5-minute car prayer, dinner check-in).

2. **Write Your Motherhood Timeline** – Reflect on who you were with each child's birth and what each season taught you.

3. **Redefine Success at Home** – What does "showing up" look like for your family? Name it. Honour it. Practise it.

Chapter 18:
The Business of Becoming You

Original Quote:

"Your business is not just what you do—it's who you are becoming."
MotivationaLee

After years of nursing, teaching, and quietly coaching, MC'ing/Hosting, Key Note Speaking on the side, the call to fully step into entrepreneurship grew louder. It wasn't just about creating another income stream or ticking a box on a career plan—it was about claiming the fullness of who I was meant to be.

The Leap From Stability to Possibility

Leaving the security of a steady nursing salary felt like standing on the edge of a cliff. I wrestled with doubts: *Could I really pay the bills? Would I lose my identity as a nurse? What if I failed?*

These fears whispered loudly, but the voice within whispered louder: *You're meant for more.*

My father's words echoed in my heart:

"As a laborer, your life evolves in your work. As an entrepreneur, your work evolves with your life."

That mindset shift was the pivot point.

Balancing Passion and Practicality

One of the blessings of my journey is that I can still nurse and teach casually, while dedicating myself to success coaching, keynote speaking, and emceeing on stage. It's not about doing everything at once—it's about intentional balance.

Learning to say *no* to opportunities that don't align with my purpose—or that stretch me too thin—has been a crucial part of that balance. I'm doing the things I love, not because they're easy, but because they bring meaning and joy.

The Pivot Point: Courage for the Change You Secretly Want

The Reality of Entrepreneurship

Starting a business is not a bed of roses. It demands investment—of time, money, energy, and heart. It's risky, calculated or not, because all businesses carry uncertainty. But fear of failure should never paralyze you. Failure isn't the end—it's a stepping stone.

Don't let self-doubt win. It kills dreams faster than any external setback ever could. If you don't take the leap, you stay stuck. You wake up in the same place, living the same day, wondering when your breakthrough will come.

Building a Business Aligned With Purpose

From day one, I knew I wanted more than profit—I wanted purpose. I wanted my business to be an extension of my core values: **empowerment, connection, courage, and authenticity**. That vision shaped the coaching programs I created, the stages I spoke on, and the workshops I led.

I embraced the learning curve—marketing, branding, financial planning. It was overwhelming, but it was also exhilarating. Saying *no* to misaligned offers, even lucrative ones, became a form of self-care and vision protection.

The Power of Authenticity

One of the hardest lessons? Letting go of the "perfect professional" mask.

I began to share my story openly—my grief, my burnout, my fears about starting over. And people didn't pull away—they leaned in. Vulnerability became my superpower.

I moved in silence and let my results make the noise. Yes, some people watched, waiting for me to fail. And that lit a fire in me—not to prove them wrong, but to prove to *myself* that I was capable. That I was already rising.

"When you are too good, they don't like it—because your growth reminds them of what they're not doing."

Not everyone claps for your growth. Some respond with envy or criticism. But you rise anyway. Envy makes people bitter when someone else gets better. But growth is not a competition—it's a calling.

Throughout my entrepreneurial journey, I chose my circle intentionally. I surrounded myself with dreamers, doers, and believers. I chose **growth over gossip. Creation over comparison.** In seven years, I discovered my real circle—those who lifted me instead of pulling me down.

Recognition That Reflects the Journey

And the fruit of that journey? Recognition—not just from clients, but from the community and beyond. In 2024 and 2025, I received several awards that affirmed my mission:

🏆 **President's Award** — Innovation Catalyst: Empowerment Advocate (Australia Council of Multicultural Entrepreneur Association)

🏆 **Victoria Top 100** — Asia Innovation Business Leader for Business Innovation & Entrepreneurial Empowerment

🏆 **Women Economic Forum** — "Iconic Women Creating a Better World for All"

🏆 **International Women's Day 2025** — Excellence in Community Empowerment & Inclusivity (Entrepreneur Business Club & Urban Vegas)

🏆 **Empowered Woman 2025 Award** — Skylark Foundation honors exceptional women leading with courage, impact, innovation, and unwavering community commitment.

🏆 **AusmumPreneur Leadership Award 2025**

Citation: Honorable mention

🏆 **International Eminence Excellence Conference**

ChangeMaker & Multitalented Women Award

The Pivot Point: Courage for the Change You Secretly Want

In recognition of my outstanding contributions and dedication to my Industry

I know my Dad in heaven is smiling. I made the pivotal shift—not with fear or doubt, but with focus and faith.

"In every adversity, focus on the grace, wisdom, and opportunity." — *MotivationaLee*

Anchored in What Matters

Today, I live a more balanced life, spending more time with my family. I've reflected deeply on what I value most. Inspired by a Kikki K journal, I wrote down my top four values:

1. Family
2. Time
3. Career
4. Stable Finances

These are interconnected. Much like in nursing: assess, plan, act—so you can meet SMART goals in life and business.

When my father passed away, I asked myself:

1. What do I value most?
2. What is the most important thing for me today?
3. What will happen if I do—or don't—act on it?

That moment of reflection set me free. Though I had no formal business background, I trusted in my capacity to grow. My parents had been entrepreneurs. The seeds were in me all along.

I believe in **neuroplasticity**. The brain rewires itself when trained. Whether it's playing piano, running a business, or speaking on stage—it's all learnable. **Consistency is the key.**

Today, I fly higher. I meet inspiring, like-minded leaders. I believe in **collaboration over competition**. We rise by lifting others. We only live once—so make it count.

The Business of Becoming You isn't just about profit margins or metrics. It's a journey of inner alignment, conscious growth, and courageous authenticity. Your business is not separate from who you are—it *is* who you are becoming.

Strategy Spotlight: Growing a Business Aligned With Your Purpose

- **Choose Alignment Over Approval** – Say no to what doesn't fit your long-term vision, even if it pleases others or brings short-term gain.
- **Invest in Self-Leadership** – Focus on mastering mindset, habits, and boundaries before scaling your business.
- **Let Your Story Speak** – Your vulnerability is your strength. It creates trust and emotional resonance with your audience.
- **Learn Loud, Move Quiet** – Stay teachable, but don't broadcast every move. Let your growth speak louder than your announcements.
- **Surround Yourself With Builders** – Choose your circle intentionally—seek out those who stretch, support, and celebrate your expansion.

Reflection Questions

- What fears or stories about "business" or "success" are holding you back?
- How can your business reflect not just *what* you do, but *who* you truly are?
- What does alignment between your purpose and work look like for you?

Key Affirmation:

"I build my business as a true reflection of my purpose, courage, and authenticity. I am becoming who I am meant to be." Motivationalee

The Pivot Point: Courage for the Change You Secretly Want

Key Takeaways

- Entrepreneurship is a journey of continual growth and alignment with your true self.
- Saying *no* is a powerful tool for protecting your energy and purpose.
- Fear and failure are natural—but self-doubt is the real obstacle.
- Your business should reflect your values, not just your skills.
- Small, consistent steps in learning and reflection create momentum and long-term impact.

Action Steps

1. **Name Your Values** – Write down three core values you want your business to embody. Reflect on *why* they matter.
2. **Say No With Purpose** – Identify one current task or opportunity to say *no* to this week. Say it kindly, but firmly.
3. **Rewrite the Fear Narrative** – List three fears or doubts. For each, write an empowering response or affirmation.
4. **Learn Something New** – Choose one small learning goal this week: read an article, watch a video, or talk to a mentor.
5. **Audit for Authenticity** – Schedule 30 minutes to assess how your business reflects your true self—and brainstorm ways to refine it.

Lee Montajes

Part Four:
Living The Pivot Life

Chapter 19:
How to Stay Rooted While You Rise

Original Quote:

"Let your roots go deep into your values, so your branches can rise high into your vision."
MotivationaLee

In every chapter of our lives, there comes a moment when we begin to rise, towards purpose, success, influence, and leadership. But as we rise, the most important question becomes: Are we rooted deeply enough not to be shaken?

When my journey as a nurse evolved into becoming a coach, keynote speaker, MC, and entrepreneur, I quickly learnt that rising too quickly without strong roots can make even the most talented person fall. I didn't want to be a shooting star, I wanted to be a deeply rooted oak tree that grows stronger with each passing storm.

The Push and Pull of Growth

There were moments when the invitations started coming in, speaking gigs, coaching clients, media features, recognition. I was finally *seen*. It was thrilling, but it was also overwhelming. I felt pulled in many directions. Some people wanted me to be someone I wasn't, more commercial, less spiritual. Some thought I should scale faster or take on every opportunity. But I had to remind myself: the success I was creating wasn't about popularity; it was about purpose.

I had to make conscious choices to stay grounded, physically, emotionally, and spiritually. Some of those decisions were hard. I had to say no to fast money if it meant losing alignment. I had to say no to people pleasing if it meant compromising my peace. I had to learn how to stay rooted, even while expanding.

I also continued my casual work in nursing and as a nurse educator, not because I had to, but because it reminded me of my roots. Serving in healthcare kept my heart humble. Teaching reminded me that empowerment is more powerful than applause.

It's easy to be carried away by ambition. But when you've spent years building something meaningful, relationships, values, inner strength, you protect it.

Staying Grounded in the Storm

There were times when the pressure to prove myself was loud. People questioned my choices, why I left a stable, full-time job with a great income. Some were waiting for me to fail. Others couldn't understand why I'd "give up" a linear path for something that looked unstable.

But I wasn't just rising, I was becoming. I held tight to my values: faith, family, integrity, and impact. I surrounded myself with people who lifted me up. I journalled every day. I prayed while driving. I reflected before making major decisions. I asked myself: Is this aligned with my bigger purpose? Will this decision feed my soul, not just my ego?

And when I felt unsure, I would go back to basics: quiet mornings with my journal, praying with my daughters, phone calls with my mum, reading scripture, listening to worship songs. These grounded me in my identity beyond achievements.

I wasn't climbing a corporate ladder anymore; I was building a life that felt rich in spirit.

Being Grounded Doesn't Mean Staying Small

Many people confuse humility with playing small. But staying grounded doesn't mean shrinking. It means knowing who you are, so you don't have to pretend to be anyone else to succeed.

I still dream big. I still make bold moves. But I don't rush the process. I trust in divine timing. I collaborate with integrity. I build with sustainability in mind. Because longevity matters more than virality.

I've seen people rise too fast and fall just as quickly. But I've also seen people, like the women in my tribe, grow with grace, discipline, and purpose. Their roots run deep. Their legacy is lasting.

I want to be one of those women.

Strategy Spotlight: Staying Rooted While Rising

- Build Depth Before Height – Focus on internal strength and clarity before chasing visibility or rapid growth.
- Protect Your Peace – Say no to opportunities that cost your alignment, even if they come dressed as success.
- Anchor Your Ambition – Let your values be the compass that guides your decisions, not the noise around you.
- Keep Purpose at the Centre – Revisit your *why* often. Growth that lasts is rooted in meaning, not metrics.
- Grow With Grace – Surround yourself with people and practices that keep you grounded in seasons of elevation.

Reflection Questions

1. Where in your life are you being called to rise right now?
2. What values keep you grounded when external success starts knocking?
3. Who or what helps you stay rooted in seasons of rapid growth?
4. Are there decisions you're making that are drifting away from your core?
5. What routines, rituals, or relationships help you return to your purpose?

Key Affirmation:

"I rise with purpose, grounded in my values. I grow strong because I am rooted deep." Motivationalee

Key Takeaways

- Staying grounded is essential to sustainable success.
- Saying *"no"* is a sacred act of self-alignment.
- Purpose-driven success requires strong values and inner clarity.
- Growth that lasts is built on foundations of integrity, humility, and vision.

- It's possible to expand without losing yourself, if you stay anchored in who you are.

Action Steps

1. Identify your top 3 values and write them somewhere you'll see every day.
2. Start a "grounding routine" (e.g., journalling, prayer, meditation, nature walks).
3. Review upcoming opportunities and say *yes* only to those aligned with your purpose.
4. Create a "Rooted While Rising" support circle, people who hold you accountable to your values.
5. Unfollow, delete, or distance from anything or anyone pulling you away from alignment.

Chapter 20:
Build a Life That Feels Good, Not Just Looks Good

Original Quote:

"Don't be fooled by the highlight reel. The real win is waking up loving the life you've quietly built."
MotivationaLee

For years, I ticked every box that looked good on paper, nursing career, stability, promotions, leadership roles, academic credentials. On the outside, everything looked polished. People would say, *"You've made it."* But behind the applause and achievements, something inside me whispered otherwise.

I remember sitting in my office as a Nurse Educator, staring at my perfectly structured calendar, and feeling like a stranger in my own life. I had respectable title, great income, a solid career path, but it no longer felt right. My soul was whispering for more. Not more *meaning*. More alignment. More joy.

It became undeniable: I wanted to build a life that *felt* good, not just one that *looked* good to others.

The Courage to Redesign Your Life

Redesigning your life doesn't come wrapped in comfort, it comes wrapped in courage. People may question your choices. You might question yourself. I certainly did.

When I stepped away from full-time employment to pursue entrepreneurship, I had moments of doubt.

Would this work?

What if I fail?

Am I too old to start over?

But I held onto one truth: this wasn't about how my life *looked*, this was about how it *felt*.

I no longer wanted mornings laced with dread. I wanted days that began with intention, not anxiety.

I wanted my work to fuel my spirit, not deplete it. I wanted to be present with my family, not just physically, but emotionally and spiritually. I wanted to serve with love, not just perform for a paycheck.

I wasn't chasing a highlight reel, I was choosing a life of *integrity* and *authenticity*.

What Does a Life That Feels Good *Actually* Look Like?

It looks like waking up with peace, not panic.

It looks like working with people who energise you, not drain you.

It looks like more time with your children than your inbox.

It looks like saying *yes* to joy and *no* to unnecessary obligation.

It looks like sitting in spaces where your soul feels seen, not just your CV.

As I transitioned into coaching, hosting workshops, emceeing events, and creating motivational content, I realised something powerful: I wasn't just building a business, I was building a life that honoured my truth.

Now, I get to work in my own rhythm. I pause when I need to. I choose projects that align with my heart. I've built boundaries that protect my peace. And most importantly, I am proud of the woman I've become, not because of what others see, but because of how I live behind the scenes.

The Real Markers of Success

True success isn't how many followers, titles, or accolades you collect. It's how you *feel* when no one's watching.

Are you at peace?

The Pivot Point: Courage for the Change You Secretly Want

Do you like who you've become?

Are you living with integrity, joy, and purpose?

Do your values align with your calendar?

Because you can have the applause of the world, but if your soul feels silenced or your joy is absent, it's time to pivot.

Choose the kind of success that feels like a deep exhale.

Strategy Spotlight: Designing a Life That *Feels* Like Success

- **Choose Alignment Over Appearance** – Stop performing for approval. Choose decisions that nourish your spirit, even if they're misunderstood by others.
- **Prioritise Peace Over Productivity** – Protect your emotional wellbeing over external achievement. Rest is a strategy, not a weakness.
- **Redefine Success for Yourself** – Your version of success doesn't have to match anyone else's. Let joy, freedom, and wholeness be your metrics.
- **Live From the Inside Out** – Build your life around what brings you meaning, not just what brings you validation.
- **Create Before You Perform** – Focus on building something real and fulfilling before you share it with the world. Your legacy starts quietly.

Reflection Questions

1. Does your current lifestyle bring you peace or pressure?
2. What does a *life that feels good* look like for you personally?
3. Where are you still performing for others instead of honouring your truth?
4. How can you shift your daily choices to reflect your values more deeply?
5. Who inspires you to live with authenticity and joy?

Key Affirmation:

*"I choose a life that reflects my heart, not just my achievements."
Motivationalee*

Key Takeaways

- True success is measured by how fulfilled, peaceful, and purposeful you feel.
- Living for validation leads to burnout; living from alignment leads to joy.
- A life that feels good often requires redefining what success looks like.
- You have the power to design a life that honours your soul, not just your status.
- Joy, freedom, and peace are success indicators too, don't overlook them.

Action Steps

1. **Journal your ideal day** – What would a fulfilling, peaceful day truly look like for you?
2. **Audit your current life** – Highlight what feels aligned and what feels forced.
3. **Say "no" to one obligation** this week that doesn't serve your heart.
4. **Add more joy** into your routine, something small that nourishes your soul.
5. **Create a "Feels Good" vision board**, not based on status, but on how you want to *feel* every day.

Chapter 21:
Reclaiming Your Power After Playing Small

Original Quote:

"You were never meant to shrink to fit into someone else's comfort zone. You were born to rise."
MotivationaLee

There was a time I caught myself dimming my light just so others wouldn't feel blinded by my shine.

I played small in rooms where I should have stood tall. I swallowed ideas. I held back questions. I over-delivered in silence and under-celebrated my own wins. Why? Because I didn't want to make others uncomfortable. I thought being humble meant hiding my greatness. I confused invisibility with humility.

Looking back now, I realise that wasn't selflessness, it was self-erasure.

For years, especially in my nursing career, I gave and gave, to patients, colleagues, the system. I poured out everything I had, often running on empty. I adapted, I adjusted, I made myself smaller in conversations, meetings, and decision-making rooms. I believed that if I stayed "pleasant" and "unproblematic," success would eventually find me.

But here's the truth: success doesn't reward silence, it responds to boldness.

I remember facilitating education sessions, speaking with passion and clarity, only to be told I was "too much." My ideas were "too innovative," my energy "too strong." So I toned it down. I quietened my fire. I second-guessed my instincts. I deferred to others, even when I knew I had the better solution.

But you can only suppress your voice for so long before the ache of inauthenticity becomes unbearable.

The Turning Point

The shift came when I launched my coaching and speaking career. Something within me cracked open. I realised the world didn't need another quiet achiever blending into the background. It needed women who showed up boldly, confidently, unapologetically.

I wasn't just reclaiming my voice, I was reclaiming my power.

With every stage I stood on, with every client I guided through breakthrough, I healed parts of myself that had once been silenced.

Because power isn't about being loud, it's about **being present.**

It's about standing rooted in your worth, even when no one claps.

It's about trusting your voice enough to use it before anyone else validates it.

And the truth? People will only recognise your power once you fully believe in it yourself.

Strategy Spotlight: Reclaiming Your Power in Real Life

- **Name the Shrink Points** – Be honest about where and why you're holding back. You can't change what you won't name.
- **Redefine Humility** – Humility isn't about making yourself small, it's about being powerful without arrogance.
- **Let Your Presence Lead** – Power isn't always loud. Sometimes it's quiet confidence, firm boundaries, and unshakable truth.
- **Stop Apologising for Your Strength** – You're not "too much." You're the right amount of *you,* fully expressed.
- **Practice Public Confidence** – Share your wins, own your expertise, and let your light challenge others to rise too.

Reflection Questions

1. In what areas of your life have you been playing small to avoid judgment or discomfort?
2. What does *reclaiming your power* look like in your current season?

The Pivot Point: Courage for the Change You Secretly Want

3. Who benefits when you shrink your potential, and who suffers when you don't step into your calling?

Key Affirmation:

"I reclaim my voice, my worth, and my space in the world. I was not born to play small, I was born to rise." Motivationalee

Key Takeaways

- Playing small doesn't protect you, it imprisons you.
- You can be humble and still stand tall in your truth.
- Reclaiming your power is a conscious choice, made one bold decision at a time.
- Your light doesn't dim others, it gives them permission to shine.
- People's discomfort is not your responsibility, your purpose is.

Action Steps

1. **Audit your life for "shrink points"**
   Identify where you've been minimising your voice, presence, or potential. Be brutally honest.
2. **Write a declaration of power**
   Craft a one-paragraph statement about the version of you who no longer plays small. Read it aloud daily.
3. **Practice being "too much"**
   Be fully yourself. Ask the question, take the lead, speak your truth, even if it feels scary.
4. **Set bold boundaries**
   Stop saying yes to avoid rejection. Say yes to *you* first.
5. **Celebrate yourself loudly**
   Post the win. Share the success. Let others be inspired, or uncomfortable. Either way, that's not your burden.

Chapter 22:
How I Found My Voice on Stage and Online

Original Quote:

"Your voice is your superpower, once you own it, you don't just speak, you shift rooms and ripple change."
MotivationaLee

Ever since I was young, I knew I was born for the stage.

In primary school, while others avoided the microphone, I gravitated towards it. Whether delivering a class presentation, competing in debates, or leading the morning assembly, something about speaking to an audience ignited a fire within me. My heart would race, not with fear, but with purpose.

I became a student leader, president of student councils, a regular face in debating clubs. With each experience, I didn't just enjoy speaking, I *thrived* in it. The quiet nods, the spark in people's eyes, the smiles of recognition... they told me: *This is where I belong.*

But even with years of experience, there were moments when doubt crept in.

Am I in the right place?

Am I good enough?

Especially after moving to the UK and travelling around Europe, I found myself shrinking in unfamiliar spaces. Surrounded by new cultures, different accents, and contrasting perspectives, I began to wonder:

What do I have to say that really matters?

Who would want to hear my voice here?

But life has a beautiful way of reminding you of your gift.

The Pivot Point: Courage for the Change You Secretly Want

I was invited to speak in diverse settings, community events, conferences, intimate workshops. And after each one, people from all backgrounds and walks of life would come up to me and say how my words moved them, inspired them, or helped them see themselves in a new light.

These weren't familiar audiences. They came from different countries, cultures, and stories. And yet, something universal happened. They felt *seen*. They felt *heard*. They felt *understood*.

That's when it clicked: **my voice was never just for me, it was a bridge.**

A bridge to help others:

- Communicate their ideas clearly and persuasively
  Listen with intention to foster deeper connection
- Speak confidently in unplanned or high-pressure moments
- Strengthen their influence through presence, energy, and emotional clarity

This wasn't just a talent anymore, it was a calling.

As time passed, I realised my voice didn't need to be confined to a physical stage.

Social media once felt like a noisy room full of comparison and judgement, but I reframed it: *It's just another stage. A different kind of microphone.*

And so, I began to show up, through posts, live videos, stories.

And with every message from a woman saying, "You spoke exactly what I needed to hear," I knew I had found my voice *online*, too.

Now, whether I'm standing in front of a live audience or sharing a reel from my living room, I know exactly why I'm speaking.

Not to impress.

Not to be perfect.

But to **empower**.

Because when *one woman* finds her voice, she gives permission for others to find theirs, too.

Strategy Spotlight: Building a Voice That Resonates

- **Reclaim Your Early Confidence** – Revisit the child or young adult in you who spoke without fear. She knew something you forgot.
- **Shift From Self to Service** – When you focus on impact over approval, the fear of judgement fades.
- **Let Your Voice Travel** – Use physical and digital stages with equal intention. Your message matters in both.
- **Turn Social Media Into a Microphone** – Don't perform, *communicate*. Let every post carry clarity, compassion, and conviction.
- **Use Feedback as Fuel** – Let audience responses remind you that your voice creates real-world ripple effects.

Reflection Questions

1. Think back to your earliest memory of speaking publicly, what did you feel?
2. What fears have silenced your voice in recent years?
3. If you fully owned your power to speak, where would you show up more boldly?

Key Affirmation:

"I was born to speak with purpose. My voice creates connection, clarity, and change." Motivationalee

Key Takeaways

- You don't need a perfect stage to speak powerfully, you need a clear mission.
- Your voice, when used with compassion and courage, becomes a tool for healing and leadership.
- Impostor syndrome fades when you shift focus from self-doubt to service.
- Speaking is more than words, it's energy, intention, and presence.

The Pivot Point: Courage for the Change You Secretly Want

- The world is always listening. What you say could be someone's turning point.

Action Steps

1. **Write your "Speaker's Origin Story"**
   Document your earliest memory of public speaking and reflect on how it shaped your voice today.
2. **Host a mini-talk**
   It could be a 10-minute Facebook Live, a short podcast, or a Zoom chat. Share your truth, unfiltered.
3. **Practice impromptu speaking**
   Choose three questions you might be asked in a panel or podcast and practise answering with clarity.
4. **Audit your digital presence**
   Does your voice show up in your content? If not, recalibrate. Let your message lead.
5. **Say yes to your next speaking opportunity**
   Even if it's small or unpaid, show up boldly. Every "yes" builds confidence and reach.

Chapter 23:
Making Peace with Your Past to Step Into Your Future

Original Quote:

"You don't have to rewrite your past, you only need to reframe it to release its grip on your future."
MotivationaLee

There was a version of me who carried the weight of every regret, every missed opportunity, and every painful word spoken in anger. She walked with her head high, but her heart was heavy, burdened by echoes of the past that lingered far louder than they should have.

That version of me was strong, but she hadn't yet discovered the power of forgiveness. Not just of others, but of herself.

Grief has a way of reshaping our identity. When my father passed away in 2017, something in me shifted. The woman who once confidently led classrooms, departments, and discussions suddenly felt untethered. I was grieving, not just the loss of my father, but a part of myself that no longer felt seen in the world I had devoted myself to: the nursing and academic system I had once loved.

For years, I had been the woman who showed up with a smile, who over-delivered, who held space for others even when her own cup was empty. But eventually, I realised that no amount of performance, no number of accolades or output, would heal the wounds I was avoiding.

I needed to pause.

I needed to confront.

I needed to forgive, and I had to begin with myself.

Making peace with your past doesn't mean denying it ever happened. It means allowing yourself to integrate it with grace.

The Pivot Point: Courage for the Change You Secretly Want

My past shaped me, the pain, the shrinking, the moments when I let others' opinions dim my light. All of it was part of the pivot. But I could no longer carry it forward in the same way.

So I began the inner work.

I journaled. I prayed. I sat with a therapist. I reflected on the woman who was silently suffering while keeping everything together. And in that sacred process, I gave her permission to evolve.

I didn't erase the story. I reframed it.

Not by pretending the pain didn't happen, but by choosing to understand it with compassion.

Every rejection, every closed door, every voice that doubted me, it was shaping me into the woman I was becoming. One who no longer stands in spite of her past, but *because* of it.

Today, I walk with peace.

I no longer need the past to make sense to anyone else, it makes sense to me. And it led me here. To a life I love. A calling I honour. A purpose that feels like home.

Strategy Spotlight: How to Make Peace With the Past

- **Stop Performing for Closure** – Not everyone will understand your journey. Don't wait for their validation to move forward.
- **Let Grief Be a Teacher** – Grief isn't a weakness, it's a sacred invitation to slow down, feel, and become.
- **Rewrite, Don't Erase** – You don't need to forget your story, just give it a new, empowering lens.
- **Forgive to Free Yourself** – Forgiveness isn't approval. It's a choice to stop carrying pain that no longer serves you.
- **Turn Wounds Into Wisdom** – The hardest chapters often contain your strongest lessons. Let them lead you forward.

Reflection Prompts

- What are you still carrying from your past that needs to be released or reframed?

- Who do you need to forgive, including yourself, to move forward with peace?
- How would your life look if you stopped letting your past define your worth?

Key Affirmation:

"I am not my past. I honour my journey, and I choose peace to lead me forward." Motivationalee

Key Takeaways

- Healing is not about forgetting the past, it's about reframing it so it no longer holds you back.
- Grief and trauma can alter your direction, but they don't have to define your destination.
- You can hold both compassion for where you've been and excitement for where you're going.
- Releasing resentment and embracing self-forgiveness are pivotal steps toward personal freedom.
- Making peace with your past clears space for you to dream again, create again, and believe again.

Action Steps

1. **Write a Letter to Your Past Self** – What do you want to say to her? What grace does she need from you now?
2. **Name the Wound** – Identify one area where you still feel stuck, and journal about what you need to let go of.
3. **Create a Release Ritual** – Burn a list of regrets, bury an object, or symbolically mark your healing journey.
4. **Reclaim Your Power** – List the lessons gained from your toughest chapters. These are your qualifications, not your shame.
5. **Seek Support** – Reach out to a coach, therapist, mentor, or trusted friend to walk beside you as you release what no longer serves you.

Part Five:
Your Turn To Pivot

Chapter 24:
The Pivot Plan – Mapping Your Path Forward

Original Quote:

"Dreams without direction are just wishes. But a pivot with a plan becomes your personal revolution."
MotivationaLee

There comes a point where inspiration alone is no longer enough. You feel the fire. You sense the shift. You can almost taste the possibility of the life you're being called to create.

But unless you move from that internal pivot into practical action, it remains just that, a possibility, not a reality.

When I left my long-standing career in nursing and education, I wasn't simply stepping into the unknown, I was designing a new path with intention. It wasn't a leap of impulse. It was a soul-led decision backed by structure, strategy, and deep self-trust.

I call it *The Pivot Plan*. Not a rigid blueprint, but a living, breathing framework. One that helped me honour where I'd been, embrace where I was going, and take aligned action towards who I was becoming.

This is how I turned the dream of becoming a coach, speaker, and entrepreneur into my daily reality.

And it all began with three powerful questions:

1. Who am I becoming?
2. What does my next chapter look like?
3. What is the next brave step I can take?

1. Define the New You

Every meaningful pivot starts with identity. You can't build a new future while clinging to an outdated self-image.

The Pivot Point: Courage for the Change You Secretly Want

For me, that meant shifting from "I'm just a nurse" to "I am a transformational speaker, leader, and coach."

I stopped waiting for permission or validation, I declared it first.

Because the world will only believe what *you* believe about yourself.

2. Get Clear on the Vision

Clarity is the fuel of courage.

I sat down and visualised my ideal life through five lenses: **Purpose, People, Prosperity, Personal Growth**, and **Peace**.

What would success *feel* like, not just look like, in each of these areas?

When your vision is clear, it pulls you forward even when motivation fades.

3. Map Micro-Moves

Massive change rarely starts with massive action. It starts with small, strategic steps, done consistently.

I broke my vision into tangible milestones: enrolling in a coaching course, building my brand *MotivationaLee*, showing up online, booking my first speaking engagement, writing this very book.

Momentum is built micro-step by micro-step.

4. Set Up Support Systems

No one pivots alone, nor should they.

I built my support circle intentionally: mentors, masterminds, prayer partners, and accountability buddies.

They helped anchor me when fear whispered too loudly or when I doubted my direction.

Your environment must support the elevation you're working toward.

5. Track, Tweak, and Trust

Your plan is not a contract, it's a compass.

I checked in monthly, adjusted goals, and celebrated small wins.

Most importantly, I learnt to *trust* the process.

The path won't always be linear, but your growth will always be leading you somewhere meaningful.

Strategy Spotlight: Turning a Pivot Into a Plan

- **Start With Identity, Not Goals** – Your pivot isn't just about what you'll do, it's about who you're becoming.
- **Vision Before Strategy** – Without a compelling vision, no strategy will stick. Map where your heart wants to go.
- **Progress in Micro-Moves** – Think small and consistent, not big and perfect. Momentum is built daily.
- **Protect the Pivot** – Surround yourself with people who get it, support it, and hold you accountable to it.
- **Adapt as You Grow** – A strong plan can evolve. Allow space for change without losing sight of your purpose.

Reflection Prompts

- What version of yourself are you stepping into?
- What does your ideal life look like in five years, physically, emotionally, spiritually, and professionally?
- What are three micro-moves you can take this week toward your pivot?

Key Affirmation:

"I am the architect of my future. Every step I take is building the life I was born to live." Motivationalee

Key Takeaways

- Clarity of identity is the foundation of every meaningful pivot. A vision without a plan is just a dream. Small, intentional steps make your pivot real.
- Your Pivot Plan should reflect your values and desired lifestyle, not just your goals.
- Community and accountability accelerate growth and offer vital emotional safety.

The Pivot Point: Courage for the Change You Secretly Want

Flexibility doesn't mean failure; it's how purpose evolves with wisdom and experience.

Action Steps

1. **Craft Your Pivot Vision Board** – Use images, quotes, and symbols that represent your next chapter. Display it somewhere visible.
2. **Design a 90-Day Pivot Plan** – Break down your goals for the next three months across personal, professional, and spiritual categories.
3. **Identify Your Inner Circle** – List five people who uplift and challenge you, and share your pivot with them.
4. **Schedule Progress Check-ins** – Pick one date per month to review, refine, and reflect on your pivot path.
5. **Celebrate Every Win** – Keep a "Pivot Wins" journal. No matter how small, track what moves you closer to your purpose.

Chapter 25:
Faith in Action – Spiritual Anchors in Times of Change

Original Quote:

"Faith is not the absence of doubt but the courage to move forward despite it."
MotivationaLee

Change shakes us. It uproots what we know and thrusts us into the unknown.

When I reflect on my own pivot moments, from grieving the loss of my father, balancing motherhood and nursing, to stepping into entrepreneurship, I realise my faith has been my unshakeable anchor.

Faith isn't just about religion; it's about trust.

Trust in the process. Trust in yourself. Trust in something greater than you.

It's the quiet, persistent voice that says, *"You can do this,"* even when the noise of fear and uncertainty tries to drown you out.

My Spiritual Journey Through Change

After my father died in 2017, grief pressed heavily on my heart.

At the time, I was working full-time as a nurse educator, a role that demanded so much of me physically, mentally, and emotionally. Despite the good income and professional success, I felt hollow inside. I wrestled with questions like: *Why am I here? What is my purpose? How do I keep going when the pain is this raw?*

In that season, I turned inward, to faith and spiritual practice. I started small: morning prayers in the car, journaling moments of gratitude, sitting quietly in reflection.

Those simple rituals slowly built a bridge between my pain and my purpose.

The Pivot Point: Courage for the Change You Secretly Want

Faith became the lens through which I saw my life, no longer just a series of obstacles, but opportunities to grow, serve, and inspire.

Why Spiritual Anchors Matter in Transition

Transitions shake our identity. They test our resilience.

But spiritual anchors steady us. They:

- Offer meaning when everything feels uncertain.
- Provide hope when doubt creeps in.
  Create calm when life feels chaotic.
- Remind us of our courage when it's time to leap forward.

When I speak on stage or coach clients, I often share that faith, whatever it means to you, is a powerful source of strength.

You don't have to have all the answers.

You just need to believe you're exactly where you're meant to be.

And that each small, intentional step counts.

How I Nurture My Spiritual Foundation

Here are a few ways I keep my spiritual anchors strong during seasons of change:

1. **Daily Intentions & Gratitude**
   Begin your day by setting a meaningful intention. Write down three things you're grateful for. Gratitude shifts your mindset from lack to abundance.
2. **Mindful Meditation or Prayer**
   Even five minutes of silence, reflection, or prayer can centre your thoughts and calm your nervous system. It's a sacred pause to reconnect with your values.
3. **Seek Uplifting Community**
   Faith flourishes in community. Surround yourself with people who support your values, challenge your thinking, and lift your spirit.

4. **Reflect on Past Victories**
   When you're doubting yourself, look back at the times you've overcome difficulty. Let those wins remind you of your inner strength.
5. **Surrender Control**
   Letting go doesn't mean giving up. It means releasing the illusion that everything is in your hands, and staying open to divine timing and unexpected guidance.

Strategy Spotlight: Strengthening Your Spiritual Core During Change

- **Turn Uncertainty Into Inquiry** – Instead of asking "Why me?", start asking "What is this trying to teach me?"
- **Build Rituals That Ground You** – Small daily practices offer rhythm, peace, and reconnection.
- **Let Faith Lead, Not Fear** – When doubt rises, anchor yourself in what you know to be true beyond the current moment.
- **Choose Stillness Over Striving** – Sometimes, the next step is to pause, not push. Listen inwards before moving forward.
- **Honour Your Own Definition of Faith** – There's no one right way. Whether it's prayer, meditation, nature, or journaling, do what aligns with your spirit.

Reflection Prompts

- What spiritual practices bring you peace, clarity, or a sense of connection?
- When was a time your faith helped you through a difficult transition?
- How can you nurture your spiritual anchors during this current season of change?

Key Affirmation:

"I trust in the journey and embrace the strength that faith gives me to step boldly into my future." Motivationalee

The Pivot Point: Courage for the Change You Secretly Want

Key Takeaways

- Faith isn't about certainty, it's about courage in uncertainty.
- Spiritual anchors offer clarity, hope, and resilience through life's transitions.
- Daily rituals, even simple ones, can deepen your connection to your inner wisdom.
- Uplifting communities and reflections on past wins build faith-based momentum.
  Surrendering control can be the most empowering decision you make.

Action Steps

1. **Create a Daily Ritual**
   Set aside 5–10 minutes each day for a spiritual practice, whether that's journaling, prayer, or simply being still.
2. **Reach Out for Spiritual Support**
   Connect with a mentor, coach, or community that shares your values and nourishes your soul.
3. **Recall Past Faith Wins**
   Write down three times your faith carried you through, let these memories reinforce your resilience.
4. **Let Go of One Thing**
   This week, release something outside your control. Practise trusting what's unfolding.
5. **Repeat Your Affirmation Daily**
   Use your affirmation during quiet moments, especially when fear or doubt begins to rise.

Chapter 26:
The Five Saboteurs and How to Silence Them

Original Quote:

"The loudest enemy is the one inside your own mind, silence it, and you will set yourself free."
MotivationaLee

The Saboteurs I Met on My Journey

When I stepped away from nursing and into the world of coaching, speaking, and entrepreneurship, I expected resistance, but not from myself.

The greatest obstacles weren't external. They were internal. Quiet, persistent voices that sowed doubt, fear, and hesitation. Over time, I came to recognise five key saboteurs that threatened to keep me stuck.

1. Self-Doubt

This was my loudest saboteur.

Even with nearly three decades in nursing and years of coaching under my belt, I often thought: *"Am I really good enough for this?"*

"Can I succeed outside the safety of healthcare?"

I've since learnt that self-doubt isn't truth, it's a test. And it can be overcome by choosing action over paralysis and belief over fear.

2. Fear of Failure

I feared losing financial stability. I feared disappointing my family. I feared proving the sceptics right.

But failure isn't the opposite of success, it's part of it.

The only real failure is giving up before you grow.

3. Perfectionism

I wanted every talk, coaching call, or decision to be flawless.

But perfectionism paralyses. It breeds procrastination and burnout. I had to accept: *Done is better than perfect.*

Momentum lives in progress, not perfection.

4. Comparison

Watching other speakers or businesswomen who seemed more polished made me question myself.

But when I reconnected with *my* story, my heart, my authenticity, I saw the power in staying in my own lane.

Comparison steals joy, energy, and purpose.

5. People-Pleasing

As a nurse and mother, I was wired to please and care for others.

But in leadership and entrepreneurship, that same habit blurred my boundaries and drained my focus.

Learning to say *no* without guilt became a turning point in protecting my peace and power.

How I Learned to Silence My Saboteurs

Here's what helped me take back control from these inner critics:

- **Name the Saboteur**: Awareness is everything. When I caught myself spiralling, I'd name it: *"This is self-doubt."* Naming it gave me power over it.
- **Reframe the Story**: I shifted *"I'll fail"* to *"I'm learning."* Changing the language changed my energy.
- **Practice Self-Compassion**: I stopped being my harshest critic. I started treating myself like someone I love.
- **Set Boundaries**: Saying "no" became sacred, not rude. It created space for what truly mattered.
- **Celebrate Small Wins**: Whether it was a breakthrough with a client or kind feedback from a post, I learnt to celebrate every step.

Strategy Spotlight: Building Mental Resilience and Inner Mastery

- **Label Your Inner Voice** – Don't let it run wild. When the saboteur speaks, name it. Call it out so it loses its grip.
- **Shift the Narrative** – Reframe limiting thoughts with empowering beliefs that move you forward.
- **Lean Into Compassion, Not Criticism** – You don't grow by bullying yourself. Kindness builds courage.
- **Protect Your Energy With Boundaries** – Every "no" to misalignment is a "yes" to your power.
- **Track Wins Daily** – Even the smallest wins help quiet your inner critic and strengthen your confidence.

Reflection Questions

1. Which of these saboteurs tends to show up the most in your life?
2. How do these inner voices shape your decisions or actions?
3. What strategies can you try to silence or manage your saboteurs more effectively?
4. How can you incorporate more self-compassion into your daily routine?
5. What small wins can you celebrate today to build confidence and momentum?

Key Affirmation:

"I am the master of my mind. I choose which thoughts to nurture and which to release. I am capable, courageous, and worthy."
Motivationalee

Key Takeaways

- Inner saboteurs often do more damage than external setbacks.
- Awareness is the first step in reducing their power.
- Reframing your thoughts and being kind to yourself builds resilience.
- Boundaries protect your focus, energy, and purpose.
- Daily wins, no matter how small, are fuel for confidence and forward momentum.

The Pivot Point: Courage for the Change You Secretly Want

Action Steps

1. **Track Your Saboteurs**
   Keep a journal for a week. Write down any negative thoughts that arise and label the saboteur behind each one.
2. **Reframe the Thought**
   For every negative inner script, write a positive or growth-focused alternative.
3. **Practice Daily Self-Compassion**
   Each morning or night, write one kind thing to yourself, as you would for a friend.
4. **Set One Firm Boundary**
   Say "no" this week to something that drains you or doesn't align with your values.
5. **Celebrate One Win a Day**
   Whether it's finishing a task, setting a boundary, or speaking up, write it down and own it.

Chapter 27:
Small Steps, Big Shifts: How to Create Momentum

Original Quote:

"Massive change is born from microscopic steps, repeated with purpose and faith."
MotivationaLee

The Power of One Step Forward

There's a photo I cherish of my daughter learning to walk, wobbly, unsure, yet determined. One foot in front of the other. She didn't overthink it, she simply moved forward.

I return to that image often when reflecting on how *I* had to learn to walk again, not physically, but in life. After decades in nursing and years spent nurturing others' dreams, I found myself staring at a blank canvas when I finally chose to honour my own. I wanted clarity. I wanted a full roadmap. But life whispered, *"Start where you are. Take the next small step."*

And so I did.

It was those tiny, consistent actions that took me from full-time nurse educator to stage speaker, coach, and entrepreneur. I didn't wake up one day with all the answers, but I committed to showing up. One small brave step at a time.

Why We Underestimate Small Steps

We live in a world obsessed with leaps, quantum success, overnight breakthroughs, highlight reels. But what's rarely celebrated is the series of micro-moves that lead to those moments.

Here's what I've learnt:

- **They reduce resistance.** Starting small feels doable. Instead of launching a full program, I began by coaching one person.

The Pivot Point: Courage for the Change You Secretly Want

- **They build belief.** Every micro-win is proof: *You can do this.* That belief fuels the next move.
- **They create momentum.** Forward motion, no matter how small, generates energy, and that energy opens doors.

When I first set out to speak on stages, I didn't land a keynote. I spoke at community events. When I started *MotivationaLee*, I didn't have a polished website or funnel, I had a message, a mission, and the will to act.

Micro-Wins That Moved Mountains

Here are a few small steps that created big shifts in my life:

- **Posting a daily quote online.** This led to speaking invites and new clients.
- **Dedicating one hour per week to my dream.** That hour grew as clarity did.
- **Sharing my story, even when my voice shook.** Vulnerability built trust and resonance.
- **Sending a scary pitch email.** One *yes* shifted everything.

The biggest shift of all? Realising I didn't need to have it all figured out, I just needed to begin.

Strategy Spotlight: Building Momentum That Lasts

- **Start Micro, Stay Consistent** – Break down your big goal into 10-minute tasks you can show up for daily.
- **Attach to Habits** – Stack your dream action onto something you already do (e.g., journalling after your morning tea).
- **Progress Over Perfection** – Imperfect action creates real momentum, far more than perfect procrastination ever will.
- **Share for Accountability** – Tell someone your next step and let their encouragement fuel your follow-through.
- **Celebrate the Tiny Wins** – Big change is built on tiny victories. Acknowledge them as evidence you're on your way.

Reflection Questions

1. What is one dream or goal that currently feels overwhelming to you?
2. What is the *smallest possible action* you could take toward it today?
3. What's held you back from starting in the past?
4. What proof do you already have that small steps can lead to big change?
5. What would your progress look like if you committed just 15 minutes a day?

Key Affirmation:

"Each small step I take is reshaping my life. I trust in momentum. I trust in me." Motivationalee

Key Takeaways

- Small steps are often overlooked, yet they're the *true* foundation of momentum.
- Consistent action breeds confidence and clarity.
- You don't need the full path to begin, the path unfolds as you walk it.
- Every action compounds. Every step counts.
- Trusting the process is just as vital as trusting yourself.

Action Steps

1. **Identify One Small Step**
   Choose a single, manageable task (e.g., send a message, write one paragraph) and complete it today.
2. **Commit to Micro-Movements**
   Dedicate 10–15 minutes daily to your goal. Set a timer. Track it. Honour the process.
3. **Celebrate Weekly Wins**
   Each week, journal your progress. Reflect on what worked and why, even the tiniest win matters.

The Pivot Point: Courage for the Change You Secretly Want

4. **Stack Your Habits**
   Pair your goal with a habit you already do. For example, work on your dream after your morning coffee.
5. **Tell Someone**
   Share your small goal with a trusted friend or mentor. Let them cheer you on or check in with you.

You don't need to leap, you just need to move. And with each intentional step, you become the person you were always meant to be.

Chapter 28:
From Fear to Fire – Becoming Who You Were Always Meant to Be

Original Quote:

"Your fear is not the end of you, it is the fire that refines you."
MotivationaLee

The Hidden Fear Behind My Smile

On the outside, I appeared confident. Accomplished. A senior nurse. A respected educator. A woman who had it all together.

But inside? I was quietly haunted by fear.

- Fear of judgment.
- Fear of not being enough.
- Fear of leaving the familiar to follow something uncertain, my calling.

When I first felt the pull to pursue coaching and public speaking, the fear was so loud I could barely hear the whisper of my dreams. I asked myself over and over:

"Who am I to do this?"

"What if I fail?"

"What if they laugh at me?"

But here's what I learnt: You don't wait for fear to disappear. You move through it. And in the movement, you find your fire.

Fear Is a Signal, Not a Stop Sign

Fear often shows up when we're on the edge of expansion. It's not always a warning to retreat, sometimes it's an invitation to rise.

I came to understand that fear wasn't my enemy. It was my indicator that something important was about to happen.

The Pivot Point: Courage for the Change You Secretly Want

There was a moment, backstage before one of my first live speaking events, when I stood frozen behind the curtain. My heart was pounding. My hands were shaking. I wanted to run. But then I reminded myself: *This fear means this matters.*

I took a deep breath, stepped forward, and began to speak. And as soon as I did, I felt my fire. The audience responded with nods, tears, applause. That was the moment I knew, I was becoming who I was always meant to be.

My Pivot From Fear to Fire

The shift didn't happen overnight. It was built through intentional moments of courage, commitment, and clarity. These three truths helped me move forward:

1. Courage Is Built Through Action

I didn't *feel* brave at the beginning. I just kept saying yes. I showed up, even afraid. I learnt that courage isn't a personality trait; it's a decision you make again and again.

2. Fire Needs Friction

You grow most when you're stretched. Discomfort became my training ground, not something to fear. I stopped avoiding resistance and started embracing it as part of the process.

3. Your Fire Is Your Voice

Every time I shared my story, whether with one person or one hundred, I ignited something inside myself and others. I realised my voice wasn't just a gift for me. It was meant to set others free too.

Strategy Spotlight: Transforming Fear into Fuel

- **Name the Fear, Then Challenge It** – What is the fear really saying? Is it true?
- **Lean Into What Scares You Most** – Often, your next breakthrough hides behind what feels terrifying.
- **Take Micro-Actions in the Direction of Fear** – One bold move can recalibrate your mindset.

- **Let Fear Be the Signal, Not the Driver** – Let it guide your growth, not control your decisions.
- **Use Your Voice as Fire** – Speak your truth, even if it shakes. It strengthens with use.

Reflection Questions

1. What fear have you been avoiding that might actually be a signpost towards growth?
2. Can you recall a time when you did something afraid, and it worked out?
3. What would you do if fear weren't standing in the way?
4. What parts of your story are you hesitant to share, and why?
5. What is your inner fire trying to tell you right now?

Key Affirmation:

"Fear does not define me. I am fuelled by fire, guided by faith, and becoming the boldest version of myself." Motivationalee

Key Takeaways

- Fear often signals you're heading in the right direction.
- Your calling may feel scary before it feels aligned.
  Courage is built through action. Clarity comes when you move.
- The fire within you is not random, it's proof of purpose.
- Becoming your true self requires walking *through* fear, not avoiding it.

Action Steps

1. **Name Your Fear**
   Write down your top three fears, and ask what each one is trying to protect you from.
2. **Act Anyway**
   Choose one small, bold action this week that aligns with your future, even if it feels scary.
3. **Create a Power Statement**

The Pivot Point: Courage for the Change You Secretly Want

Transform a limiting belief into a declaration. E.g., "I'm not good enough" → "I am becoming, and that is more than enough."

4. **Speak Up in a 'Fire Moment'**
   Say something true in a meeting, post online, or share something vulnerable with a trusted friend.
5. **Celebrate the Courage**
   Every time you take action through fear, pause and celebrate. That's where your fire lives.

Your fear may whisper, but your fire *roars*.

You were never meant to play small. You were born to rise, to lead, to ignite.

And the world is waiting for the version of you who walks forward with fire.

This is your moment. From fear… to fire.

Chapter 29: The Power of Saying Yes to Yourself

Original Quote:

"When you finally say yes to yourself, you silence the doubts, the critics, and the old version of you that played small."
MotivationaLee

The Turning Point

There comes a moment in your life when you realise you've spent far too long waiting, for permission, for the perfect time, for validation from others.

I reached that moment at a crossroads: continue playing it safe, or step fully into the woman I knew I was meant to be. I had followed the rules, excelled in my profession, earned the title, gained the respect. But deep inside, I knew I was still playing small.

Saying yes to myself wasn't just about chasing a dream. It was about reclaiming my identity. It was a bold act of rebellion against the belief that I always had to serve others before myself.

Giving Myself Permission

I used to say "yes" to everyone else, to work demands, to colleagues, to the expectations of being a perfect mum, wife, nurse, leader, and educator. But I rarely said "yes" to me.

Then one day, I paused and asked:

"What if I stop waiting for the world to approve of my choices, and I just go?"

So, I said yes.

- Yes, to my creativity.
- Yes, to slowing down when I needed to.
- Yes, to the calling I had buried for years, speaking, coaching, mentoring, creating impact.

The Pivot Point: Courage for the Change You Secretly Want

That one "yes" became the spark that reignited my soul. I realised that saying yes to yourself is not selfish, it's sacred. And when you do it, you give others permission to do the same.

The Inner Shift

The moment I truly said yes to myself, I noticed something powerful shift inside.

I stopped negotiating with fear.

I stopped shrinking just to fit into rooms that couldn't hold the fullness of who I was becoming.

And guess what?

The moment I committed, life responded.

Opportunities aligned.

The right people showed up.

Clarity sharpened.

Courage bloomed.

Saying yes didn't make things perfect or easy. But it meant I had finally chosen *me*, my growth, my truth, my mission.

Strategy Spotlight: Saying Yes with Intention

- **Notice Where You Hesitate**: What are you saying "no" to that your heart longs for?
- **Give Yourself Permission in Writing**: A visible affirmation reminds your subconscious who's in charge.
- **Start Small and Meaningful**: Even 10 minutes of "yes" to yourself daily can rewire old beliefs.
- **Track the Evidence**: Let every positive outcome reinforce that self-trust is your superpower.
- **Speak Your Shift Aloud**: Your voice matters. Saying it out loud helps you embody the new identity.

Reflection Questions

1. What area of your life are you still waiting for permission to grow in?
2. What does saying *yes* to yourself look like today?
3. What fears or beliefs are holding you back from prioritising your dreams?

Key Affirmation:

"I give myself full permission to grow, expand, and rise. Saying yes to myself is a gift to the world." Motivationalee

Key Takeaways

- Saying yes to yourself is the first step toward authentic alignment.
- Self-permission is more powerful than waiting for external validation.
- You can't serve others fully until you honour your own calling.
- When you stop playing small, you make room for your greatness.

Action Steps

1. **Write Yourself a Permission Slip**
   Literally write down: *"I give myself permission to…"* and list five things you've been holding back on. Post it where you'll see it often.
2. **Practice Intentional Yes's**
   Every day for one week, say "yes" to one small thing that supports your growth, rest, creativity, movement, learning, or setting a boundary.
3. **Create a "Yes Journal"**
   Track the shifts, outcomes, and emotional wins that come from saying yes to yourself. Let this build momentum and confidence.

The Pivot Point: Courage for the Change You Secretly Want

4. **Reframe Self-Prioritisation**
   When guilt creeps in, remind yourself: *"My growth benefits everyone I serve."* Saying yes to yourself models what self-respect looks like.
5. **Share Your Shift**
   Tell someone you trust about a time you recently said yes to yourself. Inspire them to do the same, impact begins with your story.

Chapter 30:
Becoming the Leader of Your Own Life

Original Quote:

"When you stop waiting for someone to lead you, you'll discover the power to lead yourself, and that's when life truly begins."
MotivationaLee

For the longest time, I believed leadership required a formal title, head nurse, department chair, coach, speaker. I thought it was about hierarchy and control. But through the many pivots in my life, from clinical nurse to educator, from speaker to entrepreneur, I discovered something far deeper.

True leadership begins within.

It's not about authority. It's about authenticity. It's not about directing others. It's about directing your own life, with clarity, courage, and conviction.

Becoming the leader of your own life is one of the most profound and empowering shifts you can make. It's about reclaiming your personal power. It's about moving from a life of reaction to one of creation. It's the moment you decide you're no longer just surviving, you're thriving, building, shaping, influencing.

I remember the moment everything changed. It was after a powerful coaching session where my mentor asked:

"Why are you waiting for someone to choose you? Why not choose yourself?"

That question cut through years of people-pleasing, perfectionism, and self-doubt. I had always waited to be noticed. To be validated. To be promoted. But leadership doesn't wait. Leadership *initiates*.

That shift in mindset helped me stand taller in rooms where no one else looked like me. It helped me speak up when my voice still trembled. It gave me the strength to advocate for others *and* for myself.

The Pivot Point: Courage for the Change You Secretly Want

As a woman, a mother, a migrant, and a leader, I've learnt that leading yourself means:

- Knowing your core values and aligning your decisions with them.
- Saying **no** to things that don't serve your purpose.
- Saying **yes** to opportunities that stretch your growth.
Trusting your intuition, even when others can't see the vision yet.
- Holding your vision steady, especially when no one else understands it.

Redefining Leadership on Your Own Terms

Being the leader of your own life doesn't mean going it alone, it means choosing who surrounds you with intention. You no longer wait to be saved, promoted, or acknowledged. You rise, build, speak, and grow on purpose.

Even in business, the biggest transformation wasn't creating something external, it was building the *internal* courage to lead myself. To take risks. To begin again. To rewrite old stories. To redefine leadership as something heart-led, human, and honest.

True leadership begins in the mirror. When you stop outsourcing your worth, your fire ignites. When you own your vision unapologetically, the world makes room for your rise.

Strategy Spotlight: Leading From Within

- **Own Your Decisions**: Stop waiting for consensus. Leaders listen, but they *decide* with clarity.
- **Check Your Alignment**: Is your calendar reflecting your values? If not, adjust with intention.
- **Stand in Your Story**: You don't need to have it all figured out, but you do need to own where you're going.
- **Lead Loudly or Quietly, but Authentically**: Leadership doesn't have one volume. Lead in a way that honours *you*.
- **Reframe Leadership**: It's not about titles. It's about *impact*. You are already influencing those around you.

Reflection Questions

1. In what areas of your life are you still waiting for permission?
2. What would stepping into self-leadership look like for you today?
3. What values are non-negotiable for the leader you are becoming?
4. Who inspires you to lead your life boldly, and why?
5. What limiting beliefs must you release to lead from your power?

Key Affirmation:

"I am the leader of my life. I act with courage, decide with clarity, and rise with purpose." Motivationalee

Key Takeaways

- Leadership begins by leading yourself, not just others.
- Stop waiting for validation or promotion, choose yourself. Align your actions with your highest values.
- Surround yourself with people who elevate your vision.
- Build your dream, even if no one else sees it yet.

Action Steps

1. **Lead One Area Today**
   Identify one area of your life where you've been waiting, take one bold, intentional step forward today.
2. **Write a Personal Mission Statement**
   Define what you stand for. Use it as your compass for future decisions.
3. **Reframe Three Limiting Beliefs**
   Take three old beliefs and rewrite them into empowering truths.
4. **Set Weekly Alignment Time**
   Schedule a check-in each week to assess how aligned your actions are with your goals.
5. **Practice Purposeful Boundaries**
   Say **no** to what drains you and **yes** to what fuels your vision.

Conclusion:
The Life That's Been Waiting for You

"There comes a moment in every journey when the path behind you makes sense, not because it was easy, but because it shaped you."

Every detour, delay, disappointment, and divine disruption has prepared you for the life that's been waiting for you all along. This book was never just about *my* pivot. It was written to give you permission to begin your own.

You may have seen glimpses of yourself throughout these pages, the burnout you hid behind your smile, the identity lost in a job title, the silent grief, the unspoken dreams, the quiet whisper that something more is calling you.

If you're still reading, let this truth sink in:

You are not behind. You are becoming.

A pivot isn't just a single moment. It's a mindset, a movement, a reconnection with who you were always meant to be. It's choosing faith over fear, alignment over approval, and progress over perfection.

You don't have to know all the steps before you begin. You only need the courage to take the next right one. You're not waiting for your life to begin, it's been waiting for *you* to say yes.

You are allowed to change.

You are allowed to want more.

You are allowed to start over.

And most of all, you are allowed to become the boldest, truest version of yourself.

If you remember nothing else from this book, remember this:

Your pivot point is not your breakdown, it's your breakthrough.

Thank you for walking this path with me. Now it's your turn. Step forward, boldly, bravely, and beautifully, into the life that's been waiting for you all along.

I'm cheering you on.

With love and purpose,

Lorilee Perez Montajes

Author, Coach, Speaker, Founder of MotivationaLee

Acknowledgments

Writing *The Pivot Point: Courage for the Change You Secretly Want* has been a deeply personal and transformative journey. I am immensely grateful to everyone who walked alongside me, whether for a season or a lifetime.

To Geoff, Ryan, my Mum-Evelyn, my children, Izzy, Yumi, and Lauren, your love and light fuel my purpose every day. Thank you for your patience, your joy, and for inspiring me to become the woman I am.

To my late father, Antonio Paner Perez, your unwavering belief in me continues to guide my steps beyond the physical realm. You remain my greatest champion.

To my mentors, colleagues, friends, and the incredible community of entrepreneurs and coaches who have challenged, encouraged, and celebrated me, thank you for your wisdom, your truth, and your belief in my message.

To every client and audience member who trusted me with their stories and dreams, your courage to pivot inspired me to share my own.

And to *you*, dear reader, thank you for choosing to embrace your journey with openness and bravery. May this book serve as a beacon of hope, clarity, and action as you carve out the life you truly deserve.

Thank you for being part of this incredible adventure.

Resources for Your Pivot Journey

Congratulations on taking the first steps toward your own powerful pivot! Remember, change is a journey, and you don't have to walk it alone.

- **MotivationaLee Coaching Sessions**

Personalised 1:1 and group coaching to help you discover your purpose, build confidence, and create a plan to pivot boldly in your life and career.

- **Speak to Sell Program**

Learn how to communicate with impact, influence your audience, and confidently sell your ideas, while staying true to your voice.

- **MotivationaLee Workshops & Webinars**

Live interactive sessions focused on mindset, leadership, confidence, and personal transformation.

- **Online Community & Support**

Connect with like-minded individuals on similar paths. Share your wins, your pivots, and your breakthroughs in a safe, encouraging space.

- **Website & Social Media**

Visit www.motivationalee.com for blog articles, video content, and updates.

- **HerMic**

HerMic is a branch business of MotivationaLee founded by Lorilee "Lee" Montajes

It is a premium training and empowerment platform that helps multicultural women—especially mothers—become confident, professional MCs, Moderators, and public speakers.

Follow HerMic on **Facebook**, **LinkedIn**, **Instagram**, and **TikTok** for daily motivation, live Q&As, and resources to support your journey.

HerMic Community:

https://hermic.com.au/application

Helpful Tools & Communities

Communities:

- Women's leadership groups and entrepreneur networks
- Local personal development meetups
- Online forums for pivoters and career-changers

The Pivot Point: Courage for the Change You Secretly Want

Apps & Tools:

- *Day One* or *Journey* for daily journaling
- *Habitica* or *Streaks* for habit tracking
- *Calm* or *Headspace* for mindfulness and stress relief

Remember: These tools are here to support you, but it's your courage, clarity, and commitment that create real transformation.

About the Author

Photo: CTO L Raf Serrano of Raf Serrano 1

Lorilee Perez Montajes is a seasoned Registered Nurse with 29 years of experience, including 17 years as a Nurse Educator. After decades of service in healthcare, Lee followed her calling to become a Success Coach, Keynote Speaker, Author, Professional MC and Entrepreneur, empowering others to step boldly into their life's pivots.

With a background that blends science, education, and storytelling, Lee has reached thousands through her dynamic coaching programs and powerful storytelling. Awarded multiple recognitions for innovation, community empowerment, and leadership, Lee embodies the courage to pivot and the grace to inspire others.

As a mother of three and an advocate for balance and purpose, her message centres on courage, clarity, and connection, encouraging others to release fear, embrace transformation, and create a life that reflects their true calling.

The Pivot Point: Courage for the Change You Secretly Want

Photo: CTO L Raf Serrano of Raf Serrano 2

Connect with Lee Montajes

Website: www.motivationalee.com

Facebook: @Motivationalee

LinkedIn: Lee Montajes

Instagram: @Motivationalee

TikTok: @Motivationalee

www.ingramcontent.com/pod-product-compliance
Lightning Source LLC
Chambersburg PA
CBHW061220070526
44584CB00029B/3908